Practice makes perfect.

THE MANAGER'S POCKET GUIDE TO

DOCUMENTING
EMPLOYEE
PERFORMANCE

by
Terry L. Fitzwater

HRD Press
Amherst, Massachusetts

Publisher and/or author make no warranties, express or
implied, with respect to this book and neither assumes any
responsibility for any legal complaint or action occasioned by
following its guidelines. The user assumes all risk and liability
whatsoever in connection with the use of or reliance upon the
materials contained herein and there are no oral agreements or
understandings or warranties collateral to or affecting the
understanding implicit in the purchase of this book.

Mr. Fitzwater's book is not intended to provide legal advice, and
it should not be viewed as a substitute for obtaining legal
advice. You should always contact an attorney familiar with
employment law to ascertain the lawfulness and legal
ramifications of disciplinary actions.

© 1998 by Terry Fitzwater

Published by:

HRD Press
22 Amherst Road
Amherst, MA 01002
1-800-822-2801 (U.S. and Canada)
413-253-3488
413-253-3490 (fax)
www.hrdpress.com

ISBN 0-87425-447-7

Cover design by Eileen Klockars
Editorial and production services by Mary George

 PRINTED IN CANADA

This book is dedicated to Barbara, my wife, for her support in all my endeavors and dreams.

My gratitude to John Skonberg at Littler, Mendelson for his friendship and support in reviewing this material, and to Bob Carkhuff at HRD Press for recognizing the potential of this subject matter and thinking enough of my approach to publish it.

TABLE OF CONTENTS

Foreword

Employment law in today's world is ever more complex and is continually changing. It is a climate which makes it difficult for employers to know what to do in each situation. While no one can guarantee a safe, totally defensible course of action each and every time, there are some formats to follow to improve one's chances of demonstrating to others, e.g., the courts and arbitrators, what the company did and why the company did it. This book will help you clarify and satisfy those goals.

Terry Fitzwater has written a comprehensive guide that is easily understood, is an effective roadmap to discipline, and can be implemented immediately. His process should help any organization change unwanted, unproductive behaviors before they become potential legal issues.

John Skonberg
Attorney
Littler, Mendelson
San Francisco

Preface

THIS GUIDEBOOK acknowledges the efforts of any manager tasked with giving constructive feedback. If you are such a manager, I salute you, for conducting a performance-related feedback session is one of the more difficult tasks confronting management today. It is not made any easier by our litigious society, where even an employee who is non-compliant to explicit instructions, and thus terminated or denied a promotion, can seek legal redress.

The guidebook will not prevent indiscriminate legal actions. Its primary purpose is to help you develop a process to change unwanted work be-haviors before they become a major problem. If the system works, there will be no need to concern yourself with legal action. You will have productive employees. If an employee does not respond to your efforts, you will have a well-documented defense should you find yourself a party to legal action.

What you will learn herein is an effective process of discipline and documentation. Some features of it I learned as an executive in human resources; some I developed out of necessity as the times and legislation changed doctrines and approaches. It is a process with a proven track record, one I am pleased to share with you.

Introduction

DISCIPLINE. The mention of it sends many managers, *good* managers, into a panic. I can't tell you how many times in my career I've had conversations about the topic with my management. They usually would go something like this:

Manager: *Terry, I need to say something to Jim. His performance just isn't up to par.*

Me: *What are you going to tell him?*

Manager: *That's why I'm here. I don't know where to start—how to say it to him. I'm afraid of tripping on my own words. I don't want to say anything that's going to come back and bite me, or get the company into trouble.*

Me: *Honesty is the best policy. As long as you're upfront and tell it like it is, you'll be performing your job responsibly. That's the best advice I can give you.*

Manager: *Fine. You can help with that. One other thing. What do I write? How do I document this thing? I remember*

> *you once saying that poor
> documentation is worse than none.*

Me: *Yes, I did say that. And it's true. Now
      let's see what you have to do.*

Do the concerns of this manager sound familiar?
Have you ever been at either end of a similar conversation? If so, then you probably have asked
yourself the all-too-common question, *How can
managers become more comfortable with, and more
knowledgeable about, administering discipline and
documenting disciplinary issues?*

This guidebook will provide you with an answer to
that question and help you ease the panic. Use it
as a basis for training and practice, the keys to the
preparation and confidence needed by any manager faced with disciplinary concerns.

The Purpose of the Guidebook

My intention here is twofold:

1. To instruct leadership in a positive, proactive
    approach to discipline, one that emphasizes
    behavioral modification and corrective action.

2. To equip leaders with a process for docu-
    menting performance issues, including
    suggested language and formats to use in
    documentation.

That purpose is backed by guidance for establishing these necessities:

- Clear delineation of positive expectations and deliverables
- Employee self-discipline through a performance enhancement plan, or PEP
- A PEPTALK method for gaining employee agreement
- Development of a coaching leadership style
- An understanding of a performance process to isolate factors for improvement
- Identification and implementation of legal processes for investigation and termination
- A system of due process

HOW TO USE THE GUIDEBOOK

Everything in this book is essential to your understanding of legal, effective discipline and documentation. You need to follow *all* the chapters and *every* step of the processes and formats they describe. *Do not skip a section.* Doing so could undermine the impact on the employee or weaken your case should you find yourself involved in some kind of legal action.

Remember above all that you are using these processes to work toward *positive change.* This should be a consistent message when you are giving employees the constructive feedback they need.

✦ The Five R's of Change ✦

This simple formula informs the disciplinary approach you will learn in the following chapters. It underscores the need to view discipline as positive change—a perception integral to the successful use of this book.

- ✓ **R**ecognize the problem and act on it early.
- ✓ **R**elate the issues to the employee in a problem-solving mode.
- ✓ **R**etool to resolve the problem through behavior modification or skills training.
- ✓ **R**einforce the reality of the situation by providing constant feedback.
- ✓ **R**eestablish your relationship with the employee; be readily available.

THE EMPLOYER AUDIT TO ASSESS LIABILITY

An important preliminary to using the guidebook is the completion of the following worksheet, "Employer Audit to Assess Liability." A "no" response to any question signals the need for you to investigate your organization's current methods for dealing with the issue in question. For example, if your answer to "Do you suspend before termination of employment?" is "No," then you should find out how termination is currently handled, as your organization may not be able to demonstrate due process (more about due process will be explained in Chapter 1). Your answers will provide you with a good measure of your potential vulnerability on the legal front. The more "no" responses you have, the greater your risk of indefensible actions.

The Audit Team

I suggest that you assemble an audit team and charge it with the responsibility of investigating negative findings and recommending changes. A good format for the audit work would present each problem finding followed by the recommendations. Here is an example:

Question Receiving Negative Response:
Do new hires sign a form acknowledging they have read and understand the employee handbook?

Recommendations:
— Establish a new-hire signing policy.
— Place at the end of the manual a signature block acknowledging receipt and understanding of handbook.
— Human resources will place signed document in employee's file.

Even if you answer "Yes" to most of these questions, you should use an audit team to ensure you are following through as intended. Be sure to audit yourself at least once a year to maintain your readiness.

— WORKSHEET —
EMPLOYER AUDIT TO ASSESS LIABILITY

Directions: Read the following questions and check off your answer. A "no" response signals the need for you to investigate company methods.

QUESTION	YES	NO
1. Do you have a formal progressive discipline system?	❏	❏
2. Is there a system to address employee complaints?	❏	❏
3. Is there a method for reviewing the language of policies and procedures?	❏	❏
4. Do you have an "at will" disclaimer?	❏	❏
5. Do you review disciplinary actions to ensure consistent application?	❏	❏
6. Do new hires sign a form acknowledging they have read and understand the employee handbook?	❏	❏
7. Do employees sign disciplinary actions and performance reviews?	❏	❏
8. Do you maintain comprehensive personnel files containing performance discussions, reviews, and the like?	❏	❏

(Continued)

— WORKSHEET —
EMPLOYER AUDIT TO ASSESS LIABILITY
(Continued)

QUESTION	YES	NO
9. Can anyone discharge an employee without a review?	❏	❏
10. Are employment agencies, managers, and supervisors trained in interviewing?	❏	❏
11. Do you suspend before termination of employment? Where investigation is necessary?	❏	❏
12. Is there a review process for long-service employees?	❏	❏
13. Does your employee handbook have a list of terminable offenses?	❏	❏
14. Do you limit those who can be used as a reference check?	❏	❏
15. Do you have a release agreement?	❏	❏
16. Is there a central office or figure to review all performance reviews for content, ratings, strength of message, and so forth?	❏	❏

(Continued)

— WORKSHEET —
EMPLOYER AUDIT TO ASSESS LIABILITY
(Concluded)

QUESTION	YES	NO
17. As an "at will" employer or one with mandatory arbitration, do employees sign a form specifically agreeing to abide by the policy?	❑	❑
18. Do you train your managers and supervisors on your discipline process?	❑	❑

Remember: Any "no" response means that you need to look into your company's methods for dealing with the issue.

Whether your answers were predominantly positive or negative, you will find this guidebook of value. It is designed to present a picture of the entire disciplinary process, not just pieces of the process. It also gives you an *updated* approach to an issue that has affected businesses and their employees since the day any business decided to open its doors.

You now know my purpose, and have an idea of how to use this book as a management tool. But a tool to do what? To help protect the company against frivolous legal actions *and* to bring about positive change. With that in mind, we'll now turn to the issue of discipline itself—what it is and what it is not—and other definitions essential to legal, effective discipline and documentation.

The Essential Definitions

WHAT *IS* DISCIPLINE? And what is documentation? If you have only a fuzzy idea of what these two concepts mean in an organizational context, don't feel bad—you're not alone. Many managers find it difficult to define the terms *discipline* and *documention* clearly, in a way that sheds light on their practical meaning in the workplace. Such difficulty is understandable; however, the lack of clarity is unacceptable, especially for anyone who wants to learn how to discipline and document legally and effectively.

This chapter addresses the problem by focusing on the essential definitions you need in order to fully learn and use the processes and formats to come. Specifically, we will look at these six terms:

1. *Discipline*
2. *Discussion*
3. *Documentation*
4. *Coaching*
5. *Due Process*
6. *Employment at Will*

A useful worksheet, "The Manager's Coaching Self-Profile," is also included, to help you gauge your strengths and developmental needs in the area of coaching.

1. DISCIPLINE

The word *discipline* has many meanings, some more positive than others. Most managers who panic at the thought of administering discipline do so because they immediately zero in on the word's negative associations. This limited view is unfortunate, particularly when we consider that the root of *discipline* is the Latin *discipulus,* which means "learner." Hardly a negative! And entirely important to our understanding of discipline's practical application in the workplace.

Because there is so much misunderstanding about this word's meaning in an organizational context, let's take a moment to review the dictionary definitions of *discipline* and to clarify just what workplace discipline *is not.*

The Dictionary Definitions

The basic definitions appear below (see *Webster's New World Dictionary,* Third College Edition). The elements most significant to us are highlighted in bold italics.

Discipline is . . .

- A branch of knowledge or *learning*
- *Training* that develops *self-control*, character, or orderliness and *efficiency*

- Strict control to enforce obedience
- **Self-control** or orderly conduct
- Acceptance of or submission to authority and control
- A **system** of rules
- Treatment that **corrects** or punishes

What Discipline Is Not

Of all the things *discipline* does *not* mean in the workplace, the following are the most important.

Discipline is not . . .

- Chastisement
- Embarrassment
- Ridicule
- Enforcement of a rigid chain of command

I cannot stress enough how such measures have no place in the organizational use of discipline. They create an environment in which it is virtually impossible for manager and employee to challenge each other for the betterment of all parties involved, including the department, work unit, and company. Moreover, they can lead into unproductive discussions, create a hostile environment, and cross the border into illegal action.

Remember: *Never* use discipline to chastise, embarrass, or ridicule people; and *never* use it to enforce a rigid chain of command. We want discipline to support a positive work environment, not to create a negative one.

What Discipline Is

Some of you familiar with discipline know there is a school of thought that discipline is not punishment. You will note I left it off of the list of what "discipline is not." I did so for a reason. While discipline is not intended to punish, it can be viewed as such by employees, especially in the later stages of the process. Let's face reality; termination is punishment no matter how you label or package it and despite your best efforts to present it in a professional matter. However, in the earlier stages, our goal is to correct issues of unacceptable behavior or performance. So, as used in this guidebook, and as should be understood in any workplace, *discipline* means behavior modification through constructive means, and more. Here is our working definition:

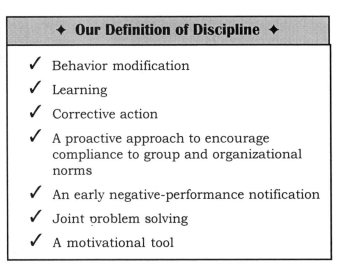

✦ Our Definition of Discipline ✦

✓ Behavior modification

✓ Learning

✓ Corrective action

✓ A proactive approach to encourage compliance to group and organizational norms

✓ An early negative-performance notification

✓ Joint problem solving

✓ A motivational tool

Always keep in mind that we want to use discipline to modify undesired behaviors *before* they become an issue. It is, in effect, an early notification system—a catalyst to manager-and-employee joint problem solving.

2. DISCUSSION

Discussion is a large part of the disciplinary process you will learn in this book. The verb *discuss* has two basic meanings, both of which play a role in the process.

1. To **speak** about something

2. To **write** about something

The "something" in this case is always the problematic issue at hand; thus discussion focuses *solely* on that issue. Put simply, the purpose of discussion is to convey to the employee, in clear and objective language, what the problem is, what behavioral changes are expected, what the employee can do to make those changes, and what action will be taken if the employee fails to make those changes.

Whether you convey this information in written or verbal form, you should be as succinct as possible, remembering the following:

- Objective comments *"describe"* the behavior.

- Subjective comments *"hide"* the behavior.

For example, the subjective comment "You have a bad attitude" cannot stand alone as a behavioral description; it is too vague. In contrast, the objective comment "Your foul language is inappropriate and unacceptable in the workplace" defines the behavior in a meaningful context; the employee knows exactly what must change, and you have an objective measure of change: the foul language will stop, or not.

In many ways, discussion is the communications bridge that helps the employee cross over into new patterns of behavior. The stronger the bridge, the greater the chance that positive change will indeed occur. Strength in this regard means clarity of expression backed by well-founded reason and objective motivation. It *does not* mean force of authority or personal aggression.

Disciplinary discussion is never an attack on the employee; nor, on the other hand, is it ever a friendly little note or chat. Managers need to encourage problem employees to change, and there is a personal element to any form of encouragement; but the issue itself must be presented in a way that emphasizes its importance. The discussion, and the issue, must have an impact on the employee's behavior.

There also is no debating *the issue*—no "pros and cons" approach to the subject as is so common in other forms of discussion. If you have reached the point where disciplinary discussion is your only option, and if you have correctly prepared for it, then debate over whether there is in fact a problem, or about the pros and cons of having to solve it, will only hinder progress toward your goal. The most fundamental message of any discussion is "There is a problem here, and it must be solved." However, keep in mind the concept of due process. Due process here is the productive exchange of information between manager and employee to effect positive change. Demonstrative "give and take," as outlined in Chapter 7, is essential in instances where an investigation is necessary.

Remember, basic reinforcement theory states that no behavior or skill will improve until someone gives the employee feedback on the performance deficiency and instruction on how to change it. Discussion is the tool by which that feedback is provided.

3. DOCUMENTATION

Documentation is the practice of formally recording, in writing, your actions and discussions throughout the coaching and disciplinary process. The resulting documents are important not only because they are a reference source for you during those processes, but also because they are your defense should a question arise about the legality of your actions.

Whenever you document—put to paper any conversations related to coaching, counseling, or discipline—you need to ensure your notes are an accurate reflection of the events, actions, and discussions that took place. Of course, this effort takes time and energy, but it is absolutely necessary if you are to discipline constructively or to ensure the integrity and safety of your workplace.

If the thought of documention usually makes your head spin, rest assured that by the end of this guidebook it will have a less dizzying effect. You will know what you need to document, especially when it comes to disciplinary matters, and how to do it; and you will have a good idea of the kind of language to use in discussion and documentation.

4. COACHING

One of the themes in this guidebook is the manager's role as a coach—a person committed to the well-being of employees, a person willing to rely on the skills and experiences of those who work for him or her. Another definition of coach: a business partner.

Coaching creates a positive work environment by building mutual trust. It means that the manager provides employees with the following:

- A committed supervisor-employee relationship

- Empowerment without fear of failure

- A listening ear and continual probing feedback to make sure messages are clear and employees understand them

- Leadership availability at all times

- Continual messages of encouragement

- Diagnoses of problems with mutual supervisor-employee solutions

A manager who acts as a coach stands a better chance of successfully disciplining a problem employee, for this kind of manager is apt to detect problems early on, to act on them quickly, and to possess the trust and respect needed to work well with the employee toward behavioral change. It is true, too, that the employee is more apt to listen when the feedback is centered on change and not on negatives perceived as punishment.

"The Manager's Coaching Self-Profile" worksheet, on the following page, will help you determine whether you are reluctant to coach or give feedback. Some managers are slightly uncomfortable with coaching; others are totally intimidated by it. Knowing your area of development need (signaled by "disagree") will get you started on strengthening them. For example, if you strongly disagree with the statement "I know how to counsel and coach," then you might try closing this knowledge gap by:

- Attending a seminar on counseling and coaching styles

- Reading this guidebook very closely

- Observing as someone skilled in coaching meets with an employee

THE MANAGER'S COACHING SELF-PROFILE				
FACTORS	**Strongly Disagree**	**Somewhat Disagree**	**Somewhat Agree**	**Strongly Agree**
I know how to counsel and coach.	❑	❑	❑	❑
I know when counseling is needed.	❑	❑	❑	❑
I'm comfortable in a counseling session.	❑	❑	❑	❑
I'm not intimidated in a counseling session.	❑	❑	❑	❑
I'm always in control of the session.	❑	❑	❑	❑
Counseling discussions get too personal for me.	❑	❑	❑	❑

5. DUE PROCESS

The principle of due process is another theme that runs throughout this guidebook. What is due process? It is a system that establishes *procedural consistency*. There are two key ingredients as it pertains to any disciplinary system.

1. The system must establish the employer's intent to objectively examine the company's philosophy of consistency concerning employee-related issues.

2. Due process must allow for employee challenges of the company's actions, that is, for right of appeal.

The disciplinary process you are about to learn, when coupled with a mechanism for employees to challenge the company's actions, will assist you with due process if honestly adopted and followed as a part of your organization's culture. We will return to the important concept of right of appeal in Chapter 3.

6. Employment at Will

In the comic strip *Blondie,* Mr. Dithers could fire Dagwood at the least provocation and get away with it. But is that the reality of today's workplace? Obviously the answer is a resounding "*No!*" The license by which bosses like Mr. Dithers could, at one time, fire any employee without cause and without due process was backed by the doctrine of employment at will. As the name suggests, this doctrine states that employment is "at the will of the employer." It has generally survived the times, and appears in some form in most policy manuals (see sample on the following page), but it does not confer the power it once did.

Sample: Employment at Will Statement

The company believes in and adheres to the doctrine of employment at will. Provisions in this manual should not be interpreted as a promise of continued employment, a guarantee of due process, or a commitment to existing terms/ conditions of employment, other than the at will employment relationship, which can only be altered by an explicit form signed by the president of the company.

Both the company and the employee have the right to terminate the employment relationship, with or without cause, at any time and for any reason.

It is important for you to know how the doctrine is worded in your company's policy manual and to be aware of any federal or state legislation that would have a bearing on the exercise of the doctrine. In both cases, they are deal *modifiers* to the doctrine. And they are guaranteed to cause any organization trouble if managers and other leaders are unaware of them or choose to ignore them.

Let's say a manager terminates an employee over the age of 40 without a good reason. A lawsuit may result even if the company has an at-will statement, because federal legislation to prevent age discrimination is unaffected by at-will employment status.

The following are some of the many modifiers to employment at will.

- Its wording in employee handbooks
- Its wording in policy and procedure manuals
- Public policy
- Americans with Disabilities Act of 1990
- Title VII—Civil Rights Act of 1964
- Age Discrimination in Employment Act of 1967 (ADEA)
- Implied contracts
  - job security
  - just cause
  - longevity
- Your own sensibilities
  - If it doesn't feel right, don't do it.

Each modifier has its own set of parameters. Unlike the parameters of legislative modifiers, company-related ones can be changed as needed. If you find, for example, that your employee handbook uses the word *permanent* to describe employees, you can and should change it. Someone could argue, and courts have agreed, that such a description sets the expectation for life-long employment. Replacing the word with *regular* is the suggested course of action. It is always a good practice to screen any documents given to employees for this and similar language that could "tie your hands" in a disciplinary situation.

Although an at-will statement is not a defense to all lawsuits, it is still a good idea to make sure it appears in your employee handbook as well as policy manual. It does set the parameters of employment and, when worded carefully, can undercut an employee's assertion he/she anticipated life-long employment, which is sometimes an issue in termination cases (an employer should make it clear that such expectations are not realistic). A good place to raise the issue is in your "offer" letter to prospective hires. Place your at-will statement in the letter. I also recommend that you have each employee sign the letter. This acknowledges that the employee has been informed of the at-will employment relationship. The issue can be revised and reinforced at a new hire orientation where they can sign a separate agreement acknowledging the at-will employment relationship.

Discipline: The Basics

HOW DO YOU KNOW when discipline is necessary? What process do you use? Are there any phases you should go through? This chapter will provide you with the answers to these and similar questions about administering discipline. They will help you build a firm foundation for dealing with problem employees and coaching behavior modification. They are your *discipline basics*.

Here are our four main areas of concern:

1. Recognizing the need for discipline

2. Utilizing a four-step process

3. Working through the phases of discipline

4. Providing quality feedback

We will look at each area in turn, covering the information you need in order to select the right approach to the problem at hand.

1. RECOGNIZING THE NEED FOR DISCIPLINE

Let's begin with a hypothetical situation. Jim, a manager in accounting, is proud of one of his hires,

Susan. She has been nothing short of excellent since he hired her 10 months ago. Jim decides she has performed so well, he'll promote her to a new position. Two months pass, and now he wonders if the promotion was such a good idea. Her work has not been error free, and in accounting, perfection is a must. He can't understand it. He mentioned the problem to her over coffee a while ago, and her response was "Don't worry, I'll get it." But her work hasn't improved. He decides to meet with her again. Perhaps discipline is the answer. Here is how their conversation goes:

> Jim: *Susan, I'm disappointed. You were coming along just great.*
>
> Susan: *I'm sorry to disappoint you. You've been a great boss.*
>
> Jim: *Am I missing something here? What can I do to help?*
>
> Susan: *I'm having some difficulty.*
>
> Jim: *What kind?*
>
> Susan: *It's my new audit job.*
>
> Jim: *But that's a great position for you. A promotion for all your hard work.*
>
> Susan: *I know, and I appreciate the opportunity. But I don't understand the audit procedures. Auditing is a lot different than accounts payable. I've never had training in some of its requirements.*

Jim is glad he had the conversation with Susan. Discipline was not the answer. He had totally missed the signals that she simply didn't know how to do the job correctly, and he could have made the situation deteriorate further with discipline. He now knows his time is better spent in *training his employee.*

This case underscores the importance of learning how to recognize the need for discipline. It also highlights two basic rules of thumb:

- Never administer discipline unless you know the employee is *choosing* not to do the job or after appropriate training still cannot perform the job adequately. Discipline is not an option if the employee cannot perform because of a lack of training or skills—**a gap in comprehension**—and is willing to learn and is capable of learning.

- Pay attention to your employees: be a coach first, a disciplinarian second. Consider the **everyday influences** that factor into *your own* behavior, such as the company rumor mill or your relationship with coworkers; keep in mind that similar influences factor into your employees' behavior too!

19

A Gap in Comprehension—or a Gap in Execution?

When confronted with an employee's performance problem, a manager first needs to determine whether the employee is experiencing a *gap in comprehension* or a *gap in execution*. Here's the difference:

- **Gap in Comprehension:** Lack of knowledge, understanding, or skill that interferes with an employee's ability to do the job as expected. A person with a gap in comprehension usually wants to perform well but *cannot* do it. He or she is in the "don't know zone."

  A gap in comprehension should not be treated as a disciplinary issue unless the employee is unwilling or refuses to learn the appropriate skills for the job.

- **Gap in Execution:** Lack of desire to do the job as expected; lack of interest in performing well. A person with a gap in execution usually has the ability to perform well but *chooses* not to do it. He or she is in the "no zone."

  An employee with a consistent gap in execution requires disciplinary action.

Whatever gap you are dealing with, you should consider the everyday influences that factor into people's behavior, and should be certain the gap is not a brief episode, before you take serious action.

FIGURE 1. Influence Factors

SOURCE	BEHAVIORAL LINKS
Organization	Culture, goals, coworkers, rumor mill, empowerment
External	Community, media, weather, unions
Home	Family, friends, illness, finances
Information	Frequency, meetings, media, strategic plans
Management's Action	Policies, procedures, training, quality of decisions, inaction, downsizings
Manager	Leadership style, supportive climate, experience, training, open-door policy

Many variables shape our day-to-day behavior

★ REMEMBER: WHEN IN DOUBT, ASK! ★

Everyday Influence Factors

It is normal for employees to have occasional gaps in comprehension and execution. The everyday influences on a person's work behavior are many and varied (see Figure 1), and they can have a significant impact on that behavior. Understanding them can help you better identify problems and resolve work issues in a timely manner.

FIGURE 2. Managing the Gap

Periods of Employee Performance

THE OPTIMAL STATE OF EMPLOYEE BEHAVIOR

Apply praise or constructive criticism as needed.

GAP IN COMPREHENSION

GAP IN EXECUTION

THE ACTUAL STATE OF PROBLEM BEHAVIOR

When lack of execution overlaps comprehension for extended periods, **consider discipline.**

GAP IN COMPRE-HENSION

GAP IN EXECUTION

"No Zone"

THE ACTUAL STATE OF PROBLEM BEHAVIOR

When lack of comprehension overlaps execution for extended periods, **provide training.**

"Don't Know Zone"

GAP IN COMPREHENSION

GAP IN EXECUTION

Remember: we all have "bad-hair days." Empathy will often go a long way in giving an employee a "lift" and setting behavior back on the routine course. Again, be a coach! When in doubt, *ask* an employee what's going on. It will save time and effort and help you identify a "behavioral link" to targeted change.

Managing Gaps in Comprehension and Execution

Normal, occasional gaps in comprehension or execution represent the "optimal" state of employee behavior. You can expect the employee to work out most issues on his or her own. However, this does not mean abdication of responsibility on your part. As a coach, you may play a role in helping the employee through praise (to keep the employee "on track") or minor constructive criticism (to put the employee "back on track"). You might also find it worthwhile to use training so these infrequent periods become authentic rarities.

Gaps of comprehension or execution that remain for extended periods represent the "actual" state of problem behavior. These "actuals" signal the need for direct supervisory action, with the use of discipline or training as interventions. Figure 2 shows the optimal state of employee behavior and the actual states of problem behavior.

Diagnosing Problem Issues

The following flow chart (Figure 3) will help you diagnose the problem at hand, pointing you in the right direction of discipline or training. Let's take a close look, moving question to question.

"Does it matter to you?"

We tend to miss this question in the discipline equation, for we often let emotions dictate our

FIGURE 3. Diagnosing Performance Issues:
Gap in Comprehension vs. Gap in Execution

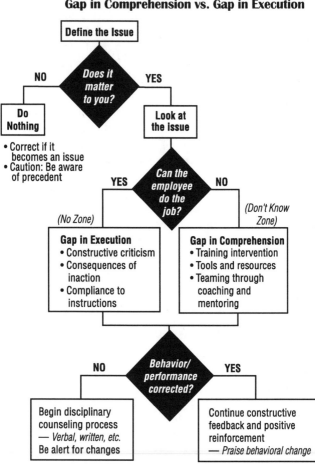

actions. We leap head-on into "fixes," not questioning or weighing the problem's relative importance. Do not let emotions prompt you to act on a trivial issue, or you will likely regret the action.

That said, it is important to remember this word of caution: triviality is in the eye of the beholder; what is trivial to you may not be trivial to someone else. As the chart warns, be aware of precedent if you answer "No" to the question and decide to do nothing. For example, if you allow a worker to return from lunch late for day-care reasons, others may view that practice as tacit approval for them to mirror the same behavior. It's difficult to argue with that logic. Also, your approval of an issue may have organizational impact if other departments point a finger and ask, "Why are they allowed to do that, but we're not?" The best way to alleviate this concern is to talk about it with your managerial associates and ask them questions. A little conversation at staff meetings can work wonders toward organizational harmony.

If the issue does matter to you, you need to *resolve the issue.* It can be accomplished simply enough by asking, and answering, the next question.

"Can the employee do the job?"

This inquiry leads us to the heart of discipline versus training. If you answer "Yes," it's time to discuss your expectations with the employee and to fully explain, through constructive criticism, the consequences of non-compliance. If you answer "No," and the job cannot be performed without the intervention of training, do not discipline. It is the manager's responsibility to provide the employee with the necessary tools for success before such action is considered.

"Behavior/performance corrected?"

If the employee has met your expectations, praise the behavior and continue providing the tools for change, whether they involve information giving, coaching, mentoring, or skills enhancement. If your expectations have not been met, begin the disciplinary counseling process, but always be on the alert for changes—look for a positive response to counseling. If you get it, be prepared to offer positive feedback to reinforce the positive change or response you expected. You may very well have worked your way out of the need for further disciplinary action.

2. UTILIZING A FOUR-STEP PROCESS

Prior to the administration of discipline, a process should be developed and institutionalized. Every employee should be advised of it and how it is used in instances of non-compliance to work expectations.

I cannot think of one organization, large or small, that does not need a process. The days of Mr. Dithers are long gone. For confirmation of this fact, you can pick up any newspaper and read about the latest million-dollar wrongful-discharge lawsuit. So if you don't have a process, develop one. I recommend a four-step process because it allows enough time for change, enough time for due process. If your company currently has a disciplinary system of less than four steps, you may want to rethink the system in light of the doctrine of due process. However, if you have less than four steps but multiple substeps for each major step, you're probably fine. The question important for you to answer is, "Can I demonstrate the employee had ample time for change?"

The Rationale for Using a Step Process

I recommend you use the step process for virtually all disciplinary actions (consider exceptions only if you are dealing with serious infractions such as fighting and theft). The rationale is simple: judges, arbitrators, review boards, and employees want to see it. A step process is useful for two primary reasons:

- It demonstrates a pattern of prolonged instances of non-performance on the part of the employee.

- It demonstrates the company's positive efforts toward change at present and over an extended period of time.

Both help protect the employer should the employee eventually be terminated and seek legal redress.

Labeling the Process Steps

How you label each step is up to you. The process labeling I find most effective is shown in the first

FIGURE 4. Sample Process-Step Options

OPTION 1	OPTION 2
1. Verbal ⌉ 2. Written ⟩— *Discussion* 3. Final ⌋ 4. Discharge/Termination	1. Verbal ⌉ 2. Written ⟩— *Warning* 3. Final ⌋ 4. Discharge/Termination
OPTION 3	OPTION 4
Step 1 Step 2 Step 3 Discharge/Termination	Step A Step B Step C Discharge/Termination

option in Figure 4. Notice the use of the word *discussion*. Some systems use the word *warning*. While *warning* will get the desired attention, it sends the wrong signal. The purpose of discipline is to change unwanted behavior, not to chastise.

A Word About Suspension

In each of these samples, suspension is an option. I recommend it in any progressive step system, no matter how you label the steps. To suspend, you send the employee home for a specified period of time, not to exceed five days. A good rule of thumb is to use a three-day period. Suspension allows the company time to investigate serious infractions such as fighting, sexual harassment, theft, and drug use or sale. It gives you time to prove or disprove allegations and deal with any lingering issues and doubts. It also allows cooler heads to prevail in these difficult situations.

When do you use suspension? At any time, and at any stage, when an investigation is necessary. It can be used whether or not the employee has a clear record or is on a final.

A Word About Documentation

It is imperative to document your actions at each step of the disciplinary process—verbal, written, and final. As mentioned earlier, your documents are valuable references for you during the process *and* your defense should any legal problem arise.

Later we will look more closely at the specifics of documentation; for now, commit to memory the all-important direction, *Document!*

Deciding on Time Allowances

The disciplinary process should allow time for improvement, hence the need for several steps. The timing between steps will vary depending on the seriousness of the performance issue. The time must be viewed as adequate for what you have established as part of the skills change or learning. For example, if employees normally produce 20 widgets a week, your performance goal should not exceed that number; otherwise, you may give the appearance of setting the employee up for failure.

Discipline Variability

One essential goal in the discipline process is consistency. However, discipline is variable. Decisions to discipline are shaped by:

- The kind of system in use
- The training one receives in the disciplinary process
- The length of employee service
- Circumstances
- Individual judgment

We will examine such variables in more detail in Chapter 3. For now, the point to keep in mind is:

30

— EXERCISE —
THE CASE OF JOHN WASASTAR

Directions: Read the following case; then circle the dates on which you would issue, respectively, a written discussion, a final, and a recommendation for discharge.

CASE: John Wasastar

John is a distribution employee with three years of average service. He has never had a performance issue, although you can remember one day when he didn't call in sick according to company policy. Two weeks ago he transferred from the second shift to the first shift. Almost immediately he started coming in late to work. Thus far he's been tardy six times in the first two weeks.

When you spoke to him about it, he told you he's been having car-pool problems and difficulty with the time difference between second and first shift. You issued a "verbal" even though he said, "All I really need is time to adjust."

TARDY RECORD

	1	2	3	4	5	6	7	8	9	10	11	12	13	14	15
JAN		L	L				L	L		L			L	L	
FEB	L		L		L		L	L	L		L		L		L
MAR				L		L			L		L	L	L	L	
APR	L		L		L			L	L						
MAY		L	L		L			L	L		L		L		

John was between 5 and 15 minutes late on each date marked "L." You issued a verbal on January 10. When do you take further action? (Circle the dates as directed above.)

If *x* occurs, *y* may happen—the result can vary on a case-by-case basis.

The exercise, "The Case of John Wasastar," illustrates this point. No two people who work on the exercise will end up with identical results. Note that a five-month time frame—from January to May—is used in the case. Most managers will terminate within that length of time if an employee does not improve the problematic behavior. If, in applying this exercise to your own company, you need more months, you can add them.

3. WORKING THROUGH THE PHASES OF DISCIPLINE

The effective approach to discipline comprises five phases, all of them equally important. They are similar to guidelines, offering you a method that begins at the first sign of trouble and ends with change evaluation. The following should be used at each step of the four-step process discussed earlier.

Phase I. *Search for the facts*
— Investigate

Phase II. *Consider possible actions or alternatives*
— Deliberate

Phase III. *Take the most appropriate action*
— Adjudicate

Phase IV. *Document*
— Administrate

Phase V. *Follow Up*
— Investigate

Phase I. Search for the Facts

This is the information-gathering phase. In most cases, you will know the whos, whats, whens, and hows of the problem. If not, you will need to investigate the situation, looking for any facts you do not have. Serious issues, such as fighting or sexual harassment, are usually complex and require a formal investigation, including solid research to establish the facts. We will look at an investigative process later on, in Chapter 7.

Investigate—The Guidelines

When searching for the facts about performance issues, be sure to do the following:

✓ **Speak with the employee.** Find out the rationale behind his or her behavior.

✓ **Review employee records.** Does the employee have prior infractions? Is this repeat behavior?

✓ **Review disciplinary guidelines**. What rules apply to the problem?

✓ **See how the rules have been enforced over time.** What precedent has been established? How have the rules been applied in similar situations?

✓ **Speak with others who know about the situation**. Are there extenuating circumstances connected to the situation? What don't *you* know about?

✓ **Discuss the issue with any former supervisors of the employee**. Is the problem repeat behavior?

✓ **Document! Document! Document!** Record your actions and the information.

The Importance of Precedent

Whether you are dealing with performance problems or more serious issues, *you should always find out how an organizational rule or guideline has been used in the past.* This is called **precedent**, and it can be an eye-opener. *Do not ignore it.*

Precedent not only gives you specific examples of how others have enforced rules or followed guidelines, but also supports any actions you take based on those examples. It may give you ideas for how to deal with the problem at hand, or confirm the legitimacy of the specific course of action you already have in mind.

Phase II. Consider Possible Actions or Alternatives

This is the "I need to think about this rationally" phase. Ask yourself the following:

- What do the facts say?

- Am I comfortable with what was stated to me and by whom it was stated?

- Did I take into consideration past friendship with the person as well as past differences? (Either could color or hide the facts.)

- Is the action I am about to take consistent with company policy, the disciplinary process, and precedent?

Here is the ultimate litmus test for determining your overall level of comfort with your decision. Ask yourself: "How would a jury or arbitrator react upon review of the company's action?"

Deliberation—The Guidelines

When considering possible actions or alternatives, be sure to do the following:

✓ **Piece the facts together.** You have your information; now see what picture you get from it.

✓ **Consider relationships of sources.** Do friendships or unprofessional working relationships taint the findings?

✓ **Weigh actions in relation to the disciplinary guidelines.** Look at whether the punishment "fits the crime." Make sure the action you are about to take is appropriate considering the offense and the disciplinary guidelines.

✓ **Determine an appropriate action plan.** Ask yourself: what must I detail and communicate to the employee to gain agreement to change? How should I do it?

Phase III. Take the Most Appropriate Action

You will need to document the actions you are taking and your expectations for the future. You can use either a disciplinary action form or a letter format for this purpose—they have the same requirements (we will look more closely at this in Chapter 5). You must detail your conversations, documenting what happened at each step. Never assume that a conversation is itself sufficient. The spoken word can be forgotten or refuted later on; written documents preserve what has been said, and they are difficult to refute. Also, keep in mind that discipline is confidential. Only those with a need to know should see the documentation.

Be aware that termination must be reviewed. Your "checks and balances" process should never allow anyone to terminate an employee without proper review, whether Human Resources or some other source is charged with the responsibility.

Adjudicate—The Guidelines

When taking appropriate action, be sure to do the following at each process step.

✓ **Obtain necessary approvals**. Most organizations require a "one over one" (approval by the reviewing supervisor's supervisor) for action at the verbal and written stages. As final discussion is the step preceding termination, and thus a serious move, you need to involve a department head, legal counsel, and Human Resources. The rationale is simple: objectivity is increased exponentially when reviewed by multiple parties.

✓ **Complete all necessary records.** A copy of the disciplinary action form or letter should be filed by Human Resources.

✓ **Meet with the employee**. Discuss the action you will take, your expectations for improvement, and follow-up actions and requirements.

Phase IV. Documentation

I cannot overstate the importance of documention during all four steps of the disciplinary process.

Documents such as disciplinary action forms and letters are an organization's first line of defense in any legal action whether it be a charge of discrimination, a wrongful-discharge lawsuit, or some other context in which the company must explain its actions. Moreover, time can be an enemy rather than an ally. Your documents will help you recall your actions, and why you took them, long into the future.

Here are some other reasons why you need to document your actions, including all discussions, during the process:

- To remember what you said to the employee, and what the employee said to you. This will prevent confusion and help both of you define clear, realistic, mutually acceptable goals.

- To demonstrate the setting of measurable and reasonable goals for improvement

- To demonstrate consistency of application. Your documents let employees and those outside the organization know that a process is used, and in a uniform manner.

- To demonstrate consistency and objectivity. Your documents let employees and outsiders know that everyone is treated according to the same standards, and that those standards hold firm against subjective influences such as personal emotion.

Moreover, it is an essential step to have the employee sign the documentation of the disciplinary discussion—verbal, written, or final—and to give the employee a copy of the signed document. In this way, you obtain proof the discussion *did* take place. (Later we will look at what you can do if the employee refuses to sign.) Any formal disciplinary document needs the employee's signature.

Administrate—The Guidelines

Documentation is an administrative procedure. When documenting, be sure to do the following:

✓ **Choose your words carefully**. Poor documentation is worse than no documentation. Take the time you need to be clear and specific about your actions.

✓ **Make sure you are comfortable with how the documentation is stated**. You may have to defend your statements. Keep in mind that the document may be subject to the legal process of discovery.

✓ **Ask the employee to sign all formal disciplinary documents, and give the employee a copy of the signed document.** As we have seen, the signed document proves the disciplinary discussion—verbal, written, or final—did in fact take place.

✓ **Keep all of your investigative or informal coaching notes.** These act as
good backup and memory joggers; but be
aware that they too may be subject to the
legal process of discovery. They should accurately reflect your observations, just as
the more formalized disciplinary document
should.

Don't forget these three rules:

❶ **Document!**

❷ **Document!**

❸ **Document!**

Phase V. Follow-Up

How do you know if you are having an impact on
the employee's behavior? Follow up. Of prime importance is the reestablishment of normal working
relationships. Remember: this is not personal, it is
business. Discipline's objective is the modification
of problem behaviors for the good of both the employee and the organization. Both manager and
employee need to know that and grow from it.

Your primary method of follow-up is meeting with
the employee. A face-to-face conversation not only
demonstrates your concern about the employee's

progress, but also gives the employee a chance to explain how he or she feels about the process and personal progress.

Additional methods of looking at the employee's progress include:

- Having the employee write a personal-progress report

- Discussing your perceptions with other managers who have come in contact with the employee, to see if their perceptions are similar to yours

The first approach will give you further *employee-provided* documentation. The second will help you assess your own objectivity about the issue at hand.

Evaluation—The Guidelines

When following up the disciplinary process, be sure to do the following:

✓ **Look for changes in attitude and performance.** Acknowledge the positive and correct the negative.

✓ **Decide how you will check on the employee's progress, and how often**. Set dates for meetings. Observe your employee at work. Adopt a structured approach, not a casual one.

✓ **Reestablish a normal working relationship with the employee**. Do not allow discipline to affect your work relationship.

✓ **Assess how well you did in the disciplinary meeting(s).** Identify ways to improve future meetings.

4. PROVIDING QUALITY FEEDBACK

No matter how well-structured a disciplinary process is, or how faithfully a manager follows the four-step process and its five phases, performance improvement will not occur unless the employee receives quality feedback. It is the key that unlocks the door to positive behavioral changes.

What is *quality* feedback? To address this question, let's look at feedback from the perspective of its helpfulness to others. By seeing when feedback is *not* helpful, we can better understand quality feedback—what it is, and what makes it helpful.

When Feedback Is Not Helpful—Poor Feedback

Universal statements are normally dangerous, but I think it's safe to say that every manager has received feedback on his or her performance at one time or another. But has it always been solid, constructive feedback? Probably not. I frequently ask my students and business associates about feedback. Their responses, included in the list below, likely reflect the norm in today's workplace.

Feedback is *not helpful* when . . .

- It deals with generalities; is not specific
- It neglects to offer possible solutions
- It is given in the presence of another employee
- It is dishonest
- The problem issue is treated with ambivalence or is driven by obsessive concern
- Feedback is sugarcoated or is presented as a bitter pill
- It is based on impossible-to-meet standards or expectations
- It is delivered with an authoritarian attitude

When Feedback Is Helpful—Quality Feedback

So what is quality feedback? Essentially . . .

> *Quality feedback is the clear communication of exactly what the performance problem is and what specific changes are needed to resolve the problem.*

The bottom line is, people cannot modify a problem behavior unless they know precisely what that behavior is and how it needs to change.

Also, *quality feedback is always grounded in . . .*

- Well-supported, objective assessment of the performance issue

- The established standards and practical necessities of the workplace

- Reasonable concern about the issue and respect for the employee

- Good communication skills, including clear expression and even-tempered delivery

- Honesty without emphasis on the bitter or the sweet

- Willingness to coach the employee, and communication of that willingness

- The attitude that giving good feedback is part of one's job

- The ability to be firm of purpose without being authoritarian in conveying that purpose

A BRIEF RECAP

We now know the basics of discipline, including the necessity for:

- *A four-step process,* to show due process

- *The isolation of execution versus comprehension,* to help us determine whether to use training or discipline

- *A five-phase process within each step,* to deliver consistency

- *Good documentation and quality feedback,* to track our progress and add definition to our expectations

The basics, by definition, are only the beginning. We will have to tie them together to facilitate the change we are after; we also will have to ground our actions to ensure consistency *over* time and from manager to manager. The next chapter, on the rules of administering discipline, will get us started in that direction.

Administering Discipline: The Rules

SO FAR, we have covered the essential definitions and basics of discipline. Now it is time to turn our attention to some of the ground rules that will facilitate the successful use of discipline. Many are related to, and reinforce, directives in Chapters 1 and 2; others introduce new concerns and instructions. Take the time you need to remember these ground rules. They are all necessary components of the task of administering discipline legally and effectively.

DISCIPLINARY GROUND RULES

The ground rules are categorized into the following areas:

- The Need for a Process
- The Manager's Rule of Thumb: A.C.T.
- Equal Treatment
- Communication of Disciplinary Rules
- Open-Flame Analogy
- Rule of Relevance
- Right of Appeal

Some areas provide you with a set of behavioral rules to follow, while others inform you of rules that should be adopted as part of your organization's employment policy and philosophy.

The Need for a Process

As I have mentioned earlier in this guidebook, you must have a process in place if you are to act consistently on discipline-related performance problems. This is one of the most fundamental ground rules of administering discipline. Another basic rule: Make sure anyone who is in the position to use discipline understands the process.

GROUND RULES: PROCESS

➡ Always use a standard process for administering discipline; if your organization does not have one, then develop one.

— A four-step process is recommended, including (1) verbal discussion, (2) written discussion, (3) final notification, and (4) discharge.

— The only exceptions to process are serious infractions such as fighting and drug use, which require formal investigation.

➡ Make sure those who administer discipline know the process.

48

— That includes understanding the difference between a gap in execution and a
gap in comprehension, and using
training, not discipline, for the latter.

— It also includes understanding the
manager's role as a coach or business
partner, and fulfilling that role for
employees.

The Manager's Rule of Thumb: A.C.T.

Coaching means being aware of your employees'
actions and providing timely feedback on performance problems. Example:
if someone is tardy for three
days in a row, do not raise
the issue three weeks later;
the employee will not understand the importance of the
feedback and will legitimately
question your delay. Instead,
be quick to ask the employee why he or she is
having the problem. This direct questioning may
be all you need. Only move to discipline if the
issue develops into a "John Wasastar."

> **A.C.T.**
>
> **A**lways
> **C**oach in a
> **T**imely manner

Keep in mind that your role as a coach is integral
to the disciplinary process—that throughout much
of the process, you will be drawing more than ever
on your coaching skills. So remember the A.C.T.
rule, and *act* on it.

49

Equal Treatment

Employees want to know that no one receives special allowances, that they are all being treated in a similar fashion. For instance, if two employees have tardiness problems, they shoud understand there is a work rule —"Be on time"—and that it applies to both of them equally, as well as all other employees; they should also understand that several violations of the rule will be dealt with through the disciplinary process.

Now one manager may define *several* as four instances; another may define it as five. A slight discrepancy like this is permissible—as I mentioned earlier, discipline can be variable. But the seriousness of the offense should carry equal weight from manager to manager.

Conduct Considerations: Fairness Equals Consistency

Some organizations, and discipline systems, try to draw a distinction between fairness and consistency. The belief is factors, such as length of service, merit undue consideration when handing out discipline. Do not be led into this trap. The reason is fairness, as a concept, is open to interpretation and as a result is subjective. What may be considered fair by management may be considered unfair by a jury. To protect yourself always equate the two by giving equal weight to both concepts. You can further protect yourself by eliminating fairness from your vocabulary. As an employer your goal is to *always* be consistent. The bottom line is that I would rather debate consistency of application than fairness

So here are our ground rules for equal treatment and consistency.

GROUND RULES: EQUAL TREATMENT AND CONSISTENCY

➽ Judge all by the same set of standards.

➽ Give thorough training in the standards to those who counsel or administer discipline.

➽ Apply those standards consistently and uniformly across all functions.

➽ Apply standards without discrimination or prejudgment. Keep discipline impersonal.

➽ Remember, consistency equals fairness.

Communication of Disciplinary Rules

It is very important for each and every employee to know your discipline process. The best way is to teach it. Train everyone in your four-step process, not just those who administer it, and explain how an employee will logically move through it should his or her performance not improve over time. Pass out an attendance sheet for everyone to sign. This is part of the "forewarning" portion of discipline.

GROUND RULES: COMMUNICATING DISCIPLINARY RULES

▶▶ Every employee and manager should know the rules. Publish them in your employee handbook and company policy and procedures manual.

▶▶ Train every employee and manager in the four-step process.

Open-Flame Analogy

Administering discipline is a difficult task; but if you have done your job correctly, there is little reason to avoid the action. In fact, you should treat it as an opportunity to help "turn around" an employee and save him or her from further action and possible termination.

The open-flame analogy emphasizes that the employee is the one who violated the rule or chose not to do the job right (touched the flame), and who now shoulders the responsibility for change. To the manager, discipline is an impersonal act—nothing more than a logical consequence of the employee's action.

Refer to the analogy whenever you are feeling uncomfortable with the task of discipline. It will also help you keep to the ground rules for consistency and communication, all of which give the analogy its power.

OPEN-FLAME ANALOGY

➮ A burn is *expected.* There is no question of the result when the flame is touched.

➮ There is ample *notice.* The person knew ahead of time what would happen if he or she touched the flame.

➮ The action is *consistent.* Anyone touching the flame is burned.

➮ The result is *impersonal.* The person is burned not because of personal identity, but because of his or her action.

Rule of Relevance

This is simply a statute of limitations. If an employee maintains a clear record for a pre-set period of time (e.g., one year), discipline begins again, but at the first step (verbal discussion). More serious acts, such as fighting, may call for reinstatement at later steps (e.g., final discussion). See your company's rules for applicability.

Maintain a copy of the disciplinary documentation in the personnel file (I used to recommend tossing it out, but times have changed). It can be used to show a prolonged pattern of problem behavior or non-performance should the employee be terminated at some point in the future. Seal the copy in an envelope, to reinforce for the employee your commitment to ignore it if performance improves.

Rule of Relevance

If an employee maintains a clear record consistent with a predetermined time frame, any disciplinary notice for the infraction may be disregarded. It is treated as if it did not exist and the disciplinary process begins with a verbal discussion for any new minor infraction.

You should ensure the clearly defined time frame is included in the employee's handbook and the company's policy and procedures manual. It is important to demonstrate to employees that nothing is "carved in stone" if there is positive response to constructive feedback.

Right of Appeal

Employees should be provided with a formal procedure for questioning disciplinary action, especially in a termination situation. Most successful companies state in their policy manuals and employee handbooks, "Any terminated employee will have the right of appeal to the President of the company on request. The President will review the matter and render a binding decision." I highly recommend this review. It is an example of due process in action, and a must in any disciplinary system.

Right of Appeal

If the company does not have a specific policy or provision to protect the rights of an employee, there should be a procedure the employee can follow to challenge company action.

THE GROUND RULES AS LEGAL SAFEGUARDS

The ground rules we have discussed, along with the instructions in Chapters 1 and 2, give you a far better chance of avoiding accusations of illegal actions, and of successfully arguing your case should a lawsuit develop, than do loosely structured approaches to discipline. They are precautionary measures on the legal front as well as sensible methods for behavior modification. They cannot guarantee *complete* freedom from legal action, no more than they can guarantee 100 percent success with behavior modification. But they can maximize that freedom, and that success, within realistic boundaries.

Checkpoint: Carroll Daugherty's Rules

Carroll Daugherty was a practicing labor arbitrator who emphasized the need for due process in his decisions. Other arbitrators referred to due process obligations, but he was one of the first to bring some definition to what a company had to do to satisfy it. The checklist on the next page incorporates Daugherty's "rules" as put forth in the case *Enterprise Wire Company, 46LA (Daugherty, 1966)*.

The following words and phrases get at the heart of Daugherty's rules and deserve special attention:

- *Forewarning*
  — Remember: use a step process.

- *Managerial rule*
  — Remember: there must be an avenue of appeal.

CHECKPOINT: CARROLL DAUGHERTY'S RULES

		YES	NO
❶	Did the company give the employee forewarning or foreknowledge of the possible or probable disciplinary consequences of the employee's conduct?	❏	❏
❷	Was the company's rule or the managerial rule reasonably related to the orderly, efficient, and safe operation of the business?	❏	❏
❸	Did the company, before administering discipline, make an effort to discover whether the employee did in fact violate or disobey the rule?	❏	❏
❹	Was the investigation conducted fairly and objectively?	❏	❏
❺	In the investigation, did the "judge" obtain substantial proof the employee was at fault?	❏	❏
❻	Has the company applied its rules, orders, and penalties evenhandedly and without discrimination?	❏	❏
❼	Was the discipline administered reasonably related to the seriousness of the proven offense and the record of the employee?	❏	❏

ANY NO RESPONSE SIGNALS DANGER!

- *Even application of rules*
  - Remember: check into precedent.

- *Discipline administered according to the offense.*
  - Remember: discipline should fit the issue.

Refer to this checklist whenever you enter the disciplinary procedure. If you can answer "Yes" to all of these questions, you are in good shape to proceed with your action. Any "no" answer signals the need to proceed with caution and, at a minimum, to revisit the action. However, a negative answer does not necessarily dictate non-action on the part of your company. Remember: all cases are different and your own good judgment will let you know if you are acting in what can be termed an arbitrary and capricious manner.

Turn to Daugherty's checklist whenever you need to assess your judgment and how well discipline was administered.

The Performance Counseling Session

THE PERFORMANCE COUNSELING SESSION is the most important and often least understood part of informal coaching and the more formal disciplinary process. The success of this meeting between the manager and the employee, in which verbal discussion of the issue takes place, relies on thorough preparation, the delivery of constructive feedback, active listening, and follow-up. Anyone who has effectively conducted such a meeting knows that the time and effort required by these tasks are worthwhile investments. They can mean the difference between resolving the performance issue quickly, right at the start of informal coaching, thus avoiding a move into the more formal disciplinary process.

In this chapter, we will take a look at the session's purpose, whether you are coaching informally or using the disciplinary process. We will then focus on the more formal disciplinary aspects of:

- Session preparation, format, and follow-up
- Handling feedback and reactions to it
- Working toward commitment to change

THE PURPOSE OF THE SESSION

The performance counseling session calls for you to draw on your coaching skills as well as your communication skills. You need to convey to the employee in clear and objective language . . .

- What the problem is

- What behavioral changes are expected

- What the employee can do to make those changes

- What action will be taken if the employee fails to make those changes

In doing so, you should give constructive feedback and offer as much encouragement as possible—that is where your role as a coach plays a vital part in behavior modification. You want to get the employee "in tune" with you and harmonizing on a mutually agreeable course of action. A useful term for

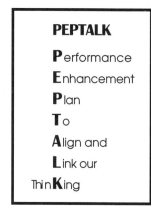

PEPTALK

Performance
Enhancement
Plan
To
Align and
Link our
Thin**K**ing

this approach is *peptalk* (see display). It will help you remember the importance of your coaching efforts throughout the performance counseling session.

It should be noted that much here is based on simple reinforcement theory. The theory has two fundamental rules:

- To increase the likelihood of someone repeating a behavior, reinforce the behavior.

- To decrease the likelihood of someone repeating a behavior, discourage the behavior.

You reinforce with praise; you discourage with criticism. In a counseling session, whether you are coaching or disciplining, that criticism should always take the form of constructive feedback—it must be a clear report of the problem backed by hard facts, sensible expectations, and useful ideas for improvement. Your intention is to change behavior, not to destroy motivation.

SESSION PREPARATION, FORMAT, AND FOLLOW-UP

1. Session Preparation

When you move from coaching to formal discipline, you "officially" place the employee in a process that could ultimately lead to termination; thus session preparation becomes very important. As we have seen, each process step has five phases:

- Phase I. Search for the Facts

- Phase II. Consider Possible Actions or Alternatives.

- Phase III. Take the Most Appropriate Action
- Phase IV. Documentation
- Phase V. Follow-Up

If you ever find yourself preparing to conduct a session "cold," without work completed on the first two phases, stop immediately. You must know the facts; and you must be sure the disciplinary process, not training, is the correct course of action.

In your preparation work, you need to focus on two things:

- The content of the disciplinary discussion and how you will document it and deliver it
- The meeting place and its environment

Anyone who has disciplined an employee knows that such discussions are usually difficult and uncomfortable. Well-planned content and a good physical setting minimize the difficulties and lend some ease to both the manager and the employee.

Content, Documentation, and Delivery

➡ **Content**

The content is simply the information you must convey to the employee. It includes the definition of the issue (the facts of the situation; the goals not being met), your expectations for the future, and the next course of action (what the employee can do to improve performance; what will happen if improvement does not occur). For a good guide, refer to the session-format table presented later in this chapter.

The number one rule here is *make good, thorough notes.* And be sure to organize your notes so you can actually work with them during the session. A few random scribbles on a piece of paper will prove useless. Remember: you are communicating serious information. Pay attention to your language; if you use general terms like *bad attitude* or *insubordination,* define them with specific examples of employee behavior. Go for the details, and know the details. Keep in mind, too, that the session requires documentation and that the employee will receive a copy of the discipline letter. Clear and well-organized notes are invaluable references in this regard and give you some assurance that you will be comfortable with the document's language and your statements to the employee.

➥ Documentation

As for documentation itself, *everything you say to the employee will need documenting.* Your organization may have a standard documentation format. If so, be ready to use it and to provide details about the session. If not, then decide what format you will use, a disciplinary action form or a letter. The content of either must reflect your conversation and detail your expectations. It is also a good practice to record, on a separate sheet of paper, what the employee said to you; statements like "Yes, I agree with your assessment" could become useful if matters go from bad to worse later on. (More information on documentation, including a sample action form, can be found in Chapter 5).

➥ Delivery

To be completely prepared for the session, rehearse your delivery of the content. This ensures you get all the issues "on the table" in a concise, effective way. Rehearsal also gives you a thorough knowledge of the material and increases your confidence.

It is also a good idea to plan for the unexpected. Think of some problems that could develop; then come up with solutions. For example, ask yourself "What if the employee gets angry and doesn't listen to the feedback? What should I do?" In this case, a list of possible solutions would include:

- Dismiss the employee until the next day to dissolve the anger.

- Suggest the employee paraphrase the feedback to calm down.

- Listen to the employee and let him or her "vent" the anger for a minute. This may diffuse the tension enough to allow you to continue.

Another Preparation Necessity!
Notifying the Employee

Let the employee know about the meeting in advance. Remember, the session calls for two-way conversation. It will be much more productive if the employee is prepared to discuss his or her perceptions of the issue. Verbal notification is fine. Here's an example:

Manager: *Jim, we need to meet on your performance. Our coaching isn't getting the results. Let's meet next Tuesday, at 9 a.m., to discuss what we can do to improve the situation.*

Jim: *Do I need to bring or prepare anything?*

Manager: *Yes. It would be helpful if you come prepared to discuss the rationale behind your inability to meet your deadlines. You know, we talked about it.*

Jim: *Okay. Thanks for letting me know. I'll make some notes.*

The Meeting Place and Its Environment

The ideal meeting place is a quiet room outside the regular work area, away from the manager's office. This kind of setting helps you informalize a formal process. It gives you the best chance of establishing the comfortable environment you need. Employees are more at ease and focused, neither anxious nor distracted by the possibility of coworkers interpreting or misinterpreting the meaning behind a closed-door meeting. Moreover, the quiet setting facilitates mutual listening and retention of information.

If you have no choice but to use an office near the work area, then be discreet. If the room has a window, close the blinds to make the space more private. Never "announce" the meeting by loudly greeting the employee, and make sure the door is firmly closed before you begin the discussion.

Before the session, take precautions against interruptions by unhooking or unplugging the telephone. Tell your secretary or assistant not to allow anyone to disturb you. Also, pay attention to the room arrangement. Eliminate artificial barriers by placing two chairs in the room's center, away from the desk. Remember, you are setting the stage for the session, and you want to create as comfortable an environment as possible.

Preparation Checklist

On the following page is a checklist of the most important items we have discussed in this section. Refer to the checklist whenever you must prepare for a performance counseling session. As a matter of note, the list is highly useful whether you are providing the employee with informal feedback and coaching, or more formal feedback and discipline. In either case, your meeting should run more smoothly and be more productive.

PREPARATION CHECKLIST

✓ Content, Delivery, and Documentation

❑ Make good, thorough notes of the information you need to convey during the session. Be prepared to detail time, places, behaviors.

❑ Be ready to document the session. If your organization does not have a documentation format, then select a format from this guidebook and use it.

❑ Rehearse your delivery; know your material.

❑ Plan for the unexpected.

❑ Give the employee advance notification.

✓ The Meeting Place and Its Environment

❑ Pick a quiet office, preferably one away from the work area and your office.

❑ "Privatize" the space. Close any window blinds.

❑ Eliminate artificial barriers in the room by placing two chairs in the room's center, away from the desk.

❑ Take precautions against interruptions. Before the meeting, unhook or unplug the phone. Make sure your secretary or assistant knows you are not to be disturbed.

❑ Never "announce" the meeting; make sure the door is closed before you begin.

2. Session Format

The session's format is structured to facilitate communication of the issue and consensus on a solution. Use the following table as your guide.

FORMAT: PERFORMANCE COUNSELING SESSION	
❶ **Begin on a Positive Note**	Put the employee at ease with positive opening statements.
❷ **Set the Agenda** • Always in private • Never discuss with other employees • Work from notes	Explain reason for meeting and whether this is an initial or repeat discussion of issue. Assure employee he or she will have time to respond.
❸ **Define the Issue(s)**	Be specific. Explain what goals are not being met.
❹ **Define Expectations**	Be specific. Define performance measures. Specify timelines for improvement. Keep expectations to the "doable."
❺ **Define Next Course of Action**	Discuss how employee can meet expectations. Explain what will happen if employee does not meet them. Work with employee to develop performance plan.
❻ **End on a Positive Note**	Set timetable for follow-up meetings. Praise positive changes. State your availability.

DOCUMENT! DOCUMENT! DOCUMENT!

This format gives you a good structure to work with—now *you* must build on it by providing the specific feedback and applying your coaching skills.

Tips for a Productive Session
The Opening. Always start the session on a positive note. Even the best feedback, improvement ideas, and action-planning attempts will go nowhere if the employee initially interprets his or her need for feedback as something negative. Your attitude, demeanor, and tone of voice should convey that the session will be dedicated to problem solving, not finger pointing or chastisement. Your opening statements should put the employee at ease and explain the session format. Here's an example:

> *Thank you for attending this meeting. I trust that you're prepared for it, and that we can have a productive, highly informative discussion. I'll begin with your work history and detail why we need to have this meeting. Please hold your comments until the end—I'll make sure you have a chance to respond to my comments. Then we'll problem-solve the issue together and create an action plan agreeable to both of us. I also want you to know that I will document this discussion and give you a copy.*

An opening like this one makes the employee feel comfortable and sets the stage for constructive work on the issue.

The Discussion. Behavior modification is virtually impossible unless you get the employee involved in performance-improvement planning. Although you alone supply the disciplinary feedback, the detailing of the problem and your expectations for change, the *problem solving* is a two-way street. A session filled solely with one-way discussion driven from the top down will yield poor results. The employee must take responsibility for the change, and will be far less likely to do that if solutions are dictated, not reached by consensus.

Closure. This should be as positive as you can make it. Praise the employee for any contributions made and any positive developments that took place. Set a time for follow-up meetings, and emphasize your availability should the employee want to see you at any time for clarification or an "unscheduled" progress report. (You can expect that most will, to demonstrate their commitment to you.) Explain that the employee will soon receive a copy of the meeting's documentation and that you will place a copy of it in his or her personnel file. Then dismiss the employee—*and start documenting.*

Here are some suggested closure statements:

- *You need to understand the impact of your actions and the consequences of your failure to comply with these instructions.*

70

- *The next course of action could lead to [specify step of disciplinary process you would take, either written or final].*

- *The next course of action could lead to further disciplinary action up to and including termination.*

3. Session Follow-Up

Follow-up reveals whether you must proceed to the next step of the disciplinary process or can consider the session a success. Select an evaluation method, and continue to provide the employee with feedback by holding follow-up meetings as planned. Be available, coach the employee as needed, and remember to reinforce with praise any improvements made by the employee. (For guidelines on follow-up, see Chapter 2, Phase V of the disciplinary phases.) Also note: if you are at the "final" step of discipline and see no improvement, your option is termination.

HANDLING FEEDBACK AND REACTIONS TO FEEDBACK

1. Handling Feedback

To convey the information needed for behavioral change, you must keep control of the session, and that means maintaining *your* self-control at all times. You will not accomplish much if the discussion turns into an argument, no matter whose fault that is. Any chance of the employee listening to feedback in the aftermath will be slim.

So, above all, hold on to the session: keep the tone business-like, and refuse to be drawn into an argument or a debate. In that way, you can achieve the goals we discussed in Chapter 2. Learn what good feedback is, rehearse it when preparing for a session, and maintain control of the session so that you can effectively use it.

The following guidelines will help you deal with feedback. In using them, keep in mind the advice "Know your audience." If you see ways to push the 'right buttons' in a person to get your point across, then push them.

Handling Feedback: Behavioral Guidelines— 4 S's

- *Sensitivity*
  - Keep the tone business-like.
  - Do not express personal feelings, concerns, or explanations.
  - Do not belittle the employee in any way.

- *Staying on course*
  - Do not make small talk.
  - Do not be led into argument or debate.
  - Keep to your script.
  - Stick to the facts.

- *Sugarcoating the message*
  - Never sugarcoat the message; you will only confuse the employee. Don't send mixed signals. Tell it like it is.

- *Situational specifics*
  - Remember the session is intended to correct performance. It is meaningful, and you and the session have purpose.
  - If the session is not going well, dismiss the employee and arrange a next-day meeting. Cool off.

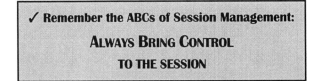

✓ **Remember the ABCs of Session Management:**

ALWAYS BRING CONTROL

TO THE SESSION

2. Handling Reactions to Feedback

Positive or Negative?

From the manager's perspective, there are really only two employee reactions to counseling: positive and negative. Of course, each can take many different forms; for example, a negative reaction can be anything from sheer apathy to outright rage. And a manager must deal with whatever form it takes. But essentially, a reaction is positive if the employee recognizes the issue and his or her strengths and developmental needs; a reaction is negative if the employee fails to recognize them or disagrees with the manager's viewpoint on them.

The table below provides you with a quick and simple reference for acting on these polarities. Note the need to focus on facts and clarity should the reaction be negative. The rule here is *act, do not react*. That is, focus on the goal of the session and the action needed to reach that goal. Do not lapse into the personal, reacting emotionally.

Basic Reaction and Action Table

Question	If so . . .	If not . . .
Does employee recognize the issue and agree with your viewpoint?	Acknowledge agreement and provide positive reinforcement.	Specifically identify and define them, and point out the issue's importance for task achievement.
Does employee recognize own strengths and developmental needs and agree with your viewpoint?	Acknowledge agreement and provide positive reinforcement.	Specifically identify and define them, and point out their importance for task achievement.
Always ask employee for suggestions. **Arrive at consensus on performance plan.**		

Empathy and Availability

Empathy is an important part of any counseling session. It is not enough to point out discrepancies and consider your job is finished; you must be available to help the employee work through any anger and disagreement with your views. Performance improvement will be the "quicker" end result.

Handling Difficult Personality Types

There are a number of different personality types, but three stand out as being particularly difficult to work with when a manager is giving feedback. They are the intimidated, the inattentive, and the argumentative.

Intimated or Inattentive. The most effective way to get through to initimated or inattentive types is by involving them in the session as much as you can. As you work through the discussion, periodically ask the employee to paraphrase what you have just said. Have the employee take notes; later in the session, ask the employee to write out his or her goals and action plan (use the Performance Enhancement Plan—PEP— form included at the end of this chapter). Doing so gives the intimidated employee confidence and draws the inattentive one into action; it also instills ownership.

The following list summarizes these suggestions and presents a few others.

Handling the Inattentive or Intimidated Employee

- Sit directly in front of the employee.

- Begin with PEPTALK. Coach the employee as much as possible.

- Have the employee take notes to build confidence or to focus attention.

- Ask the employee to paraphrase discussion.

- Ask open-ended questions to ensure understanding and encourage conversation.

- Enlist employee in action planning.

- Have employee write out goals and plans (use PEP form).

Argumentative. The argumentative person is the most difficult of the three types. The key here is to diffuse the anger. You must convey that the discipline is not personal—it is business. Avoid generalities; they feed the flames. Focus on details, and stress that the employee will have an active role in performance planning. Above all, maintain control— do not get drawn into an argument or a debate. If your attempts to diffuse the anger are clearly going nowhere, dismiss the employee and set a time to meet the next day. Time often leads to "cooler heads" and the productive exchange of information.

Handling the Argumentative Employee

- Begin with PEPTALK. Be business-like in your coaching, and avoid generalities.

- Attempt to diffuse the anger. Remind the employee this is business, nothing personal.

- Do not engage in argument or debate.

- Ask employee to recommend action for improvement.

- Have employee write goals and action plan (use PEP form).

- Reinforce with follow-up meetings.

- Dismiss employee if necessary; set time for a next-day meeting.

GAINING COMMITMENT TO CHANGE

The employee is the one who must bring performance up to acceptable standards; the manager can only supply the road map and help determine the best way to reach the destination. To facilitate commitment to change, have the employee fill out a PEP form (see next page). It is also a good way to demonstrate in any subsequent litigation that the employee knew there was a performance problem and accepted responsibility for it. Near the session close, ask the employee to complete the form. discuss its contents, modify it to the agreement of both parties, and have the employee sign it upon completion.

— FORM —
PERFORMANCE ENHANCEMENT PLAN

Please ask yourself the following questions and record your answers:

1. What are the issues we have discussed and have agreed merit my attention?

2. What can I do to improve my performance? (Discuss your goals, targeted objective[s], and timelines.)

3. How can my supervisor help me achieve my performance enhancement plan?

Employee   Date: Supervisor   Date:

Documentation

AS A PROMINENT LABOR ATTORNEY once told me, no documentation is sometimes better than poor documentation. His point: poorly worded discussions can get you in trouble. Even if you verbally discuss the issue in clear detail, serious problems can develop if the employee takes legal action and your record of that discussion is vague, incomplete, or worse—contains erroneous information or harmful statements. The approach in this chapter therefore emphasizes the language and content of documentation as well as the format.

Specifically, we will take a close look at:

- Your primary goal in documenting discipline

- Document validation

- Your documentation options: letter format or disciplinary action form

- The letter format, including outlines for verbal and written discussion

- Final discussion and its special needs

- The disciplinary action form

- The effective use of language: impact words

As termination is the final, more troublesome step of the process, its documentation (as well as its procedure) will be detailed in Chapter 6. It is a step that, if you discipline and document effectively, should lessen your concerns.

DOCUMENTING DISCIPLINE: YOUR PRIMARY GOAL

In working through this chapter, and whenever documenting the disciplinary process, keep in mind the following:

- **Clarity** *is your main goal.* The document should . . .
    - be easy to understand
    - succinctly present the facts and the supporting details of the problem
    - convey expectations for change
    - specify the consequences of non-compliance to requested performance improvement
    - set specific and achievable goals for performance improvement
    - demonstrate your company's willingness to work with the employee over a given period of time

- **_Objectivity_** _facilitates clarity._ Keep to the hard facts, describing the problem via those facts. In good documentation, nothing is subject to interpretation. If you aim to be objective, you will more easily attain your goal of clarity.

- **_Completeness_** _facilitates clarity._ Include all the facts.

For example, a problem definition such as "Your tardiness is a concern" may seem clear, but not if we compare it to this:

> _Your continuing instances of tardiness, five in the last month on January 5, 10, 21, 27,and 28, strain the productivity of the department and your coworkers, and the tardy behavior cannot continue any longer._

The employee knows that the tardiness is indeed a _problem_ and gets a _complete picture_ of that problem: it is continual; it affects others; it cannot continue. There also is little room for interpretation, filling the requirement of _objectivity_. The meaning is clear to the employee and to any third party reviewing the document. It is just what you need to strive for in your documentation efforts.

Also, notice the dates of the tardy behavior are defined. While it is not essential it is a good practice to be this specific. If you do not include the dates make sure you convey that information to the employee and retain written evidence of each incidence in the file. But, as a standard rule remember this: dates, times, and incidences will always strengthen a letter.

DOCUMENT VALIDATION

It is important to know from the start these two technicalities:

1. You must ensure the employee receives a copy of the document, no matter what step of the disciplinary process you are taking.

2. You must validate the document by obtaining proof the employee received a copy of it.

The first technicality is easy to cover. Simply give the employee a copy of any formal discussion.

The second technicality requires getting the employee to sign the original document and then giving him or her a copy of it. But what if the employee refuses to sign? Then note at the bottom of the document "Hand-delivered to [name of employee] this [date]." Either act—signing or hand delivering the document—helps to validate the document. As a matter of note, this is also the time to guarantee the document's protection by placing it in the employee's file.

OPTIONS: LETTER FORMAT OR ACTION FORM

In documenting the disciplinary meeting, you can use either a letter format or a disciplinary action form. The letter relies on you for its structure and content; you write it "from scratch," following an outline for the body of the letter. The action form offers you, to some degree, a ready-made structure; it provides basic check-off information and a fill-in area for detailing the disciplinary situation (for a simplified action form, see next page). The fill-in area demands your clear and structured input, though, just as the body of the letter does. The content will be one and the same.

The advantage of the letter format is that you can "freestyle" the format. The advantage of the action form is that it offers uniformity of format and consistency from one employee to another.

— SAMPLE —
DISCIPLINARY ACTION FORM: SIMPLIFIED

Name: Dept:
Date:

Level of warning: ❏ Verbal
                                         ❏ Written
                                         ❏ Final
                                         ❏ Discharge

Reason for discussion: ❏ Initial Meeting
                                         ❏ Continuing Issue

Nature of performance issue:

_____   _____
Employee   Supervisor

Copy to employee and personnel file

No matter which option you select, the content will vary depending on the process step you are taking. Here are the basic differences:

- *Process Step 1: Verbal discussion*
  Documentation for this step focuses on the information conveyed, and the performance-improvement plan developed and agreed on, during the performance counseling session. It is a clear, faithful record of the session.

- *Process Step 2: Written discussion*
  Documentation for written discussion focuses on unmet expectations for improvement; it reminds the employee of his or her agreement to carry out the performance-improvement plan in Step 1, and of any developments that took place in follow-up meetings. This documentation sounds a danger alarm: it lets the employee know that the next course of action will be final discussion unless change indeed occurs.

- *Process Step 3: Final Discussion*
  The content focuses on unmet expectations and plans, and reminds the employee about the previous verbal and written discussions. It details the additional reasons why the meeting was necessary. This session is a wake-up call and a last chance for the employee to live up to his or her agreements to change; there is no "next time."

THE LETTER FORMAT

In general, the disciplinary letter consists of three parts: (1) the salutation, (2) the body, and (3) the manager-employee signature area. The salutation directs the letter to the employee, the body presents the main text of the letter, and the signature area provides lines for, and identifies, the respective signatures of manager and employee.

Obviously, the body of the letter requires the most work, and the most guidance; thus it will be our focus here. Salutations and signature areas will be shown in the sample letters I have included.

Outline for Verbal Discussion

As you know by now, it is critical to document a verbal discussion—what you say to the employee, and what the employee says to you, during the performance counseling session. Don't forget: if you prepare good, thorough notes for the session, and convey their information to the employee, you will have a head start on this documentation.
When organizing the body of your letter, use the outline on the next page and the related comments that follow it.

Outline: Verbal Discussion

1. Introduction

- Date and time of meeting
- Statement of employee's need to devote attention to, and to comply with, goals "as discussed today and outlined in this letter"

2. Issue development

- Stated reason for meeting

3. Main text

- Problem/issue definition; what goals are not being met
- Description of the behavior to change; definition of expectations
- How employee can meet expectations; the performance goals and the plan that manager and employee have agreed on
- Timelines
- Course of action if objectives are not met

4. Closure

- Timetable for follow-up meeting
- Positive statement

Introduction

Writing the introduction can be a difficult task, but it is quite important because it sets the tone for the rest of the letter. Always note the meeting's date. Including the time is not crucial, but it does emphasize the significance you are attaching to the meeting and disciplinary discussion. Use it as you deem necessary.

You should always state the employee's need to pay attention to the letter's contents and to comply with the goals you will specify therein. The phrase *as outlined in this letter* is a useful modifier. For instance:

> *This letter serves to confirm our discussion concerning a work-related issue needing your immediate attention **as outlined in this letter**.*

> *Our meeting today was specifically designed to detail performance expectations for your position **as outlined in this letter**.*

Here are other examples of opening statements:

- *Today, [date], at [time], we discussed a work-related issue, outlined below, which needs your immediate attention.*

- *This letter serves to confirm your need to pay attention to, and comply with, the goals discussed today, [date], and outlined below.*

- *Per today's discussion and your agreement, the [performance] issue we discussed will receive your undivided attention.*

- *It is important for your future employment with the company that you work diligently toward the objective we set today, [date].*

- *As of today, [date], we discussed your need to improve your performance as specified below.*

- *As of today, [date], you have agreed to comply with the goals and standards set forth in this document.*

- *Your continuing attention to the work-related issues we discussed today and outlined below is necessary to demonstrate your commitment to change.*

Issue Development

You now start focusing on the issue. A general statement about the issue will prepare the way for further definition in the main text of the letter.

It is often useful to preface such statements with *per our discussion* or *as we have discussed*. This reinforces your document's legal strength because it confirms the discussion. Below are some sample development statements for cases of absenteeism, tardiness, and performance-related issues.

Absenteeism

- *This meeting was called because you must improve your overall rate of absenteeism.*

- *Your continuing absenteeism cannot be tolerated.*

- *Your failure to adhere to company standards for absenteeism is affecting your ability to meet departmental objectives.*

- *Your failure to comply with normal rates of absenteeism is negatively affecting your ability to meet your position's objectives.*

- *Your absenteeism rate is becoming a morale issue to the department.*

- *Your pattern of absenteeism is unacceptable.*

- *Your absenteeism is excessive and unacceptable, and must improve immediately.*

Tardiness

- *You must find ways to reduce your instances of tardy behavior.*

- *Your tardy rate is above the departmental average and is interfering with your job performance.*

- *Per our discussion you must find ways to control your rate of tardiness.*

- *You need to consider the impact of your tardy behavior on the department [or coworkers].*

Performance-Related Issues

- *You must develop a more thorough under- standing of the process, including [specifics of process].*

- *You must devote immediate attention to thoroughly understanding the specific job duties of your position, including [specific job duties].*

- *There are specific aspects of your position where you are not performing up to expectations, including [specific aspects].*

- *You continue to violate the company's work rule concerning [smoking, safety, extended break periods, and so forth].*

- *You must take the time to learn more concerning your assigned tasks, including [specific tasks].*

Note the repeated use of *including* in the samples for performance-related issues. This lets the employee know what the specific area of the problem is and acts as a bridge into further issue definition. A detailed example:

You must take the time to learn more about the assigned tasks, including:

(1) How to enter journal-ledger entries according to GAAP and divisional requirements.

(2) How to quickly retrieve information from the mainframe computer.

The manager who is dealing with this sample issue would detail, in the next portion of the letter (the main text), just what the specific performance problems are; for instance, that the employee's entries require constant review and that he or she spends excessive time on information-retrieval.

Main Text

This is where you focus on the specifics of the discussion—the issue definition, the goals not being met, your expectations for change, the performance plan you and the employee have agreed on, the timelines, and the course of action you will take if the employee does not improve the problem behavior. (See also page 70, Performance Counseling Format.)

Here is an example for absenteeism:

> *As we have discussed, you missed nine days of work in the past two months, on January 10, 13, 22, 25 and 27 and on February 9, 12 and 13. This rate of absenteeism is substandard according to company goals and policy, and has had a negative impact on the productivity of the department. This performance is unacceptable. To conform to company standards, you must reduce your absenteeism rate by 60 percent. According to our discussion, you have agreed to meet the company standard from this day forward and to support any absences for medical reasons with a physician's statement, which will be subject to verification. As you know, failure to meet your stated goal will result in further disciplinary action.*

You might personalize some statements by adding an opening phrase such as "Now is the time." For instance, "Now is the time for you to improve your on time performance, or we will have no choice but to place you on a written."

As mentioned earlier in the guidebook, goals should always be obtainable—they may "stretch" the employee's abilities, but should never set the employee up for failure. Your discussion of goals should focus only on what the employee can reasonably meet, and the documentation should accurately record that discussion. "Failure goals" will not motivate and are subject to intense scrutiny in wrongful-discharge litigation.

Closure

Set the timetable for follow-up meetings, and end on a positive statement. Emphasize the employee's commitment to change, and make sure the employee knows you will be available for help at any time. For instance:

- *The company expects you to make every effort to comply with the performance improvement plan we discussed and as outlined in this letter. I am confident you will make these efforts, and I am ready and willing to assist you whenever necessary.*

- *According to your stated commitment, you have agreed to work diligently toward meeting the performance objectives we discussed and as detailed in this letter. I trust you will make every effort to improve. If I can help you in any manner, please let me know.*

How does all of the above come together in the actual letter? To find out, take a look the sample document on the next page.

✦ How It All Comes Together ✦

Letter for Verbal Discussion—Sample

Intro

This letter serves to confirm your need to pay attention to, and comply with, the goals discussed today, January 6, and as outlined below.

Issue Dev.

Specifically, your failure to comply with the normal rates of absenteeism is having a negative effect on your ability to meet your position's objectives.

Main Text

This situation has had a negative impact on the productivity of the department. This performance is unacceptable. To conform to company standards, you must reduce your absenteeism rate by 60 percent. According to our discussion, you have agreed to meet the company standard from this day forward and to support any absences for medical reasons with a physician's statement, which will be subject to verification. As you know, failure to meet your stated goal may result in further disciplinary action.

Closure

This letter serves as a formal verbal discussion. The company expects you to make every effort to comply with the performance improvement plan we discussed and as outlined in this letter. I am confident you will make these efforts, and I am ready and willing to assist you whenever necessary.

Sign. Area

Manager **Date:**	**Employee** **Date:**

Outline for Written Discussion

As the written discussion is the second step of the disciplinary process, your documentation should specify the employee has not met the goals agreed to in the meeting (performance counseling session), and that further non-compliance will prompt a final. Remember: it is important to validate the document with the employee's signature to prove he or she received a copy of the document and that the meeting took place.

The outline is similar to that of verbal discussion, but emphasizes the employee's non-compliance and need to recommit to the change effort. The outline is shown on page 97.

Introduction

State present date and remind the employee of date of session. Also mention the date of any follow-up meeting. Your statement of employee's need for attention and compliance to agreed-on goals should set those goals in the context of the prior meeting and documentation of that meeting. Be sure it is clear you are *re*stating the goals here. The employee and any third party who sees this document must understand these unmet goals are a continuing problem.

Issue Development

Basically, issue development for absenteeism, tardiness, and performance-related issues is the same as the issue development for verbal discussion. For examples, see previous section on the outline for verbal discussion.

Main Text

Restate the problem definition and explain what goals the employee is still failing to meet. Review your expectations and the details of the performance plan; emphasize that the employee agreed to follow the plan and must begin to comply with that agreement. Set new timelines, and explain that final action will be taken if the goals remain unmet at those times. The main text in the sample letter on the page 98 illustrates the above.

Closure

In closing the letter, you must stress the need for the employee's recommitment to the performance plan. Always end on a positive note, reminding the employee that you are available for further help. This is important because it not only lets the employee know there is continuing managerial support, but also demonstrates to any third party that such support was offered. For an example, see the sample letter on page 98.

Outline: Written Discussion

1. Introduction

- Present date; reminder of date of prior meeting (verbal discussion) and date of any follow-up
- Statement of employee's need to devote attention to, and to comply with, goals "as agreed to during our meeting [and reinforced by any follow-up], as outlined in the record of that meeting, and as restated in this letter"

2. Issue development

- Why meeting took place

3. Main text

- Restatement of problem/issue definition; what goals are still not being met
- Restatement of the behavior to change; redefinition of expectations
- What performance goals and plan manager and employee agreed on, and that have not been met and followed
- Need for employee's recommitment to change behavior and reach stated goals
- New timelines
- Final action to be taken if goals still are not met by dates specified in timelines

4. Closure

- Emphasis on importance of compliance
- Emphasis on importance of recommitment to meet goals and follow plan
- Positive statement of continuing support

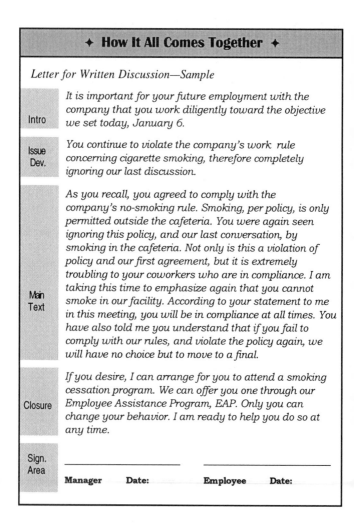

✦ How It All Comes Together ✦

Letter for Written Discussion—Sample

Intro

It is important for your future employment with the company that you work diligently toward the objective we set today, January 6.

Issue Dev.

You continue to violate the company's work rule concerning cigarette smoking, therefore completely ignoring our last discussion.

Main Text

As you recall, you agreed to comply with the company's no-smoking rule. Smoking, per policy, is only permitted outside the cafeteria. You were again seen ignoring this policy, and our last conversation, by smoking in the cafeteria. Not only is this a violation of policy and our first agreement, but it is extremely troubling to your coworkers who are in compliance. I am taking this time to emphasize again that you cannot smoke in our facility. According to your statement to me in this meeting, you will be in compliance at all times. You have also told me you understand that if you fail to comply with our rules, and violate the policy again, we will have no choice but to move to a final.

Closure

If you desire, I can arrange for you to attend a smoking cessation program. We can offer you one through our Employee Assistance Program, EAP. Only you can change your behavior. I am ready to help you do so at any time.

Sign. Area

_____   _____
Manager   **Date:**   **Employee**   **Date:**

Final Discussion and Its Special Needs

As we have seen, final discussion is the employee's last chance to alter his or her behavior before termination. It is a wake-up call and your last attempt to get through to the employee, who, for whatever reason, is clearly in a non-compliance mode. Thus effective joint problem solving takes on a heightened sense of urgency. You need to communicate that the employee must change, "or else." And yes, at this point, discipline does sound more punitive than positive.

Outline for Final Discussion

The outline is essentially the same as the one for written discussion, which you can use as a general guide. However, in your introduction, be sure to remind the employee of the previous verbal *and* written discussions. Also keep these exceptions in mind:

- The language and tone in the main text should assume a more serious nature, particularly when you are discussing the final action to be taken if goals are not met by the dates specified in the timelines.

- The closure should underscore the serious-ness of this final action.

Discussing Final Action. The following examples illustrate the kind of language and tone you need to convey the gravity of this disciplinary step.

- *Your failure to comply with the goals set in our two previous discussions leaves the company with no choice but to place you on a final.*

- *Your reluctance to deal with your performance issues, as we mutually agreed, cannot be ignored and leaves us with no option but to place you on a final.*

- *The company cannot ignore your continuing reluctance to deal with the performance issues we outlined and discussed on several occasions. You leave us with no option but to place you on a final.*

- *We have had multiple conversations about your continuing performance problems. These were acknowledged by you on the dates as recorded above. Your failure to live up to your commitment to improve necessitates the need for a final.*

Closure. So far, I have emphasized the need to close with as positive a statement as possible, one that will demonstrate your continuing support for the employee. This is still our goal, but now we must lay out in no uncertain terms the seriousness of the final action. For example:

- *John, this is your final opportunity to comply with the goals we have now discussed on three occasions. I hope you decide to do so, but you are the only person who can make that happen.*

> *I have previously stated to you, and will restate now, that I am available to help you. Your failure to comply at this point, however, must be understood. The company's next course of action is termination.*

- *You need to understand the importance of compliance at this stage of our process. Non-compliance is no longer an option, and your failure to comply will lead to termination. I have been available to help you, and I will continue to offer my support.*

Our goal with language like this is to leave no room for interpretation. In meeting this goal, you may find the employee particularly reluctant to sign the document; if so, hand-deliver it according to the instructions provided earlier in this chapter.

THE DISCIPLINARY ACTION FORM

At certain times, you may find it preferable to use an action form, rather than a letter, to document the disciplinary-process step you are taking. I personally prefer it because it adds structure, carries a formal title, and acts as a memory jogger for the various steps of the discipline process.

In this chapter's discussion of format options, you were shown a simplified version of an action form. A more detailed version appears on the following page. Select the form that best fits the issue you are dealing with.

— SAMPLE —
DISCIPLINARY ACTION FORM: DETAILED

Employee Name _____   Position _____

Division _____   Region _____

Disciplinary action to be taken:

- ❏ Performance
- ❏ Violation of Rules

Action required:

- ❏ Verbal Discussion
- ❏ Written Discussion
- ❏ Final Discussion
- ❏ Discharge

Detailed performance
improvement required:

- • Expectations   • Time Frames
- • Measurements • Consequences

Explanation of situation and action to be taken:

*I acknowledge a copy of the above
has been given to me this day.*

Date:

_____   _____
Employee   Supervisor

102

Filling Out the Action Form

Note the the three major sections of the detailed version:

- Disciplinary action to be taken
- Action required
- Detailed performance improvement required

Each is further defined, with the first two offering easy check-off of related items.

As mentioned earlier, the third, fill-in section requires your clear, thorough input. The outlines for the body of the disciplinary letter are valuable guides in this respect. Use them to craft your explanation of the situation and the performance plan you and the employee have developed and agree on. Be sure to include the following:

- Issue identification

  Example: *You have failed to meet your sales quota for the last three months.*

- Description of the behavior or issue that must change

  Example: *Your percent to plan was 92 percent in June, 88 percent in July, and 85 percent in August. This suggests a trend that cannot continue, and you must achieve plan.*

- Objectives to achieve the plan

  Example: *We discussed this issue and you agreed to call on six new customers each month, call on existing customers twice a month, and make sales presentations on the company's new products to at least 30 percent of your client base.*

- Time expectations

  Example: *You must be on plan by the end of the year.*

Remember: practice makes perfect. Use the sample forms to practice how you would document the first three steps of the disciplinary process. Review the results with someone and ask for a critique. I have included an exercise at the end of this chapter to get you started on your action-form practice.

THE EFFECTIVE USE OF LANGUAGE

I cannot stress enough that whenever you are documenting the disciplinary process, you should lead into the specifics and then focus on them. The more detailed—clear, objective, and complete—the documentation is, the better. Precise, *defensible* language is your ally here, as is language that *makes an impact* on the employee. You want to convey whatever information is needed to resolve the issue, and you want to do so in a way that sparks the employee's motivation and then continues to fuel it. Remember: the commitment to change must be intense and lasting; it has to survive the difficulties the employee may encounter later, when trying to modify his or her behavior.

Defensible Language

Defensible language means language that conveys specific, objective facts. Indefensible language is vague—subject to interpretation, indefinable without explanation. Such language is best exemplified by the two terms *bad attitude* and *insubordinate.* Managers tend to overuse them and thus unwittingly subvert the disciplinary process.

To avoid this trap, detail the observations that led to your conclusion of insubordination or bad attitude. For instance, the following describes a bad attitude: "The employee was argumentative with a customer. I directly heard him shout into the receiver, 'The shipping problem isn't my fault! What do you expect me to do?'" Such a statement adds definition and is easily understood. So be specific: detail the instances that led to your conclusion of insubordination or bad attitude, and thoroughly describe the employee's behavior.

Impact Words

Starting on page 107 is a list of words and phrases often found in good documentation. Use them to formulate sentences for your discipline and documentation efforts. Notice that some instill action, while other point toward change. They will help you clarify and detail work expectations.

To get an idea of how such impact words work in a sentence, look at these samples:

> *Together we can **search** for **alternatives** to **isolate factors** for **improvement** to **prevent** future **problematic** issues.*

> *Let's **work together** to **jointly** establish a **mutually agreeable course of action.***

> *You need to **search** for **alternatives** that will **contribute** to task **deliverables. Failure to comply** or **implement** our **agreements will result** in further **formal** action.*

> *Your **flagrant disregard** for our **mutually defined** goals continues your **prolonged pattern** of ignoring **compliance** to expected group **norms.***

> - *Our **counseling process** and our subsequent **goal setting** has **reinforced** your need to **improve** and **modify** your **unproductive pattern** of **behavior**.*
> - *We need to **work together as a team** to **improve** your **level of understanding**. You must take **ownership** in this **process** to **lessen the likelihood** of further disciplinary action.*

➡ IMPACT WORDS TO LEARN AND USE

Actions
Adversity
Agreement
Alternatives
Approach
Assist
Attention
Behaviors
Cannot
Ceased
Cessation
Change
Coach
Collaborative
Commit
Compliance
Confirm
Consequences
Consider
Consistent
Constructive
Continued
Contribute
Contributing
Control
Conversation
Cooperation
Corrective
  action

Counseling
Course of action
Critical
Deal with
Decrease
Deliver
Deliverables
Demonstrate
Detrimental
Deviate
Devise
Direction
Discharge
Disciplinary
  review
Discussion
Disobedience
Disobey
Documented
Effort
Encourage
Encouraged by
Establish
Evaluate
Exchange of
  information
Excused
Expectation
Explicit

Factors
Failure to comply
Flagrant
  disregard
Follow up
Frequency
Further action
Formal
Goal setting
Guide
Identify
Ignore
Impact
Implement
Improve
Improvement
Inappropriate
Informal
Infraction
Intolerable
Isolate
Jointly
Know
Lessen the
  likelihood
Level of
  understanding
Look for
Modify

(Continued)

IMPACT WORDS TO LEARN AND USE *(Concluded)*

Motivational
Mutually
  agreeable
Mutually
  beneficial
Mutually
  defined
Need to
Negative
Norms
Objective
Observation
Partner
Pattern
Positive
Positive
  environment
Positively
Possible
  action
Prevent
Preventive
Problem
  solving

Problematic
Process
Prolonged
  pattern
Provide
Put to paper
Realistic
Reasonable
Reduce
Reinforce
Relevant
Repeated
Repetitive
Resolution
Response
Search
Self-directed
Serious
Solutions
Specifically
Step
Stopped
Substantial
Suspend

Take ownership
Task
Termination
Think about
Timelines for
  improvement
Timing
Turn around
Understand
Understanding
Undesired
Undivided
Unproductive
Unwanted
Up to and
  including
Violation
Warning
Will not be
  tolerated
Will result
Work together
  as a team
Write it up

— EXERCISE—
DISCIPLINARY ACTION FORM

Directions: Use what you have learned so far from this guidebook to manage the case situation below. Read the case, and take some time to think about the situation; then fill out the blank disciplinary action form on the next page.

An example of good discipline and documentation practice is shown in the action-form section that concludes the exercise.

CASE: A Final for John Wasastar

John Wasastar is now in sales, and he just is not listening to your feedback. It's as if he doesn't really care. On March 4, you gave him a verbal notice, and on July 10, a written notice. He has been well aware that you've been available for help.

It's November 1, and he still is not meeting the goals you and he set to improve performance, specifically:

1. **To call on 10 new clients each quarter**

2. **To increase plan achievement by 95 percent**

3. **To complete a weekly report detailing his sales calls and interactions with customer service**

You are about to sit down with him and issue a final notice. What will you say? Take some time to gather your thoughts—make some notes if necessary. Then use the action form to record your statements. Remember, you ordinarily would be filling out this form *after* you had spoken with John, not before. (If need be, continue your explanation on a separate sheet of paper.)

(Continued)

— EXERCISE —
DISCIPLINARY ACTION FORM *(Continued)*

Employee Name _____   Position _____

Division _____   Region _____

Disciplinary action to be taken:
- ❏ Performance
- ❏ Violation of Rules

Action required:
- ❏ Verbal Discussion
- ❏ Written Discussion
- ❏ Final Discussion
- ❏ Discharge

Detailed performance improvement required:
- Expectations
- Measurements
- Time Frames
- Consequences

Explanation of situation and action to be taken:

I acknowledge a copy of the above has been given to me this day.   Date:

_____   _____
Employee   Supervisor

(Continued)

— EXERCISE —
DISCIPLINARY ACTION FORM *(Continued)*

Sample Explanation:

> **Explanation of situation and action to be taken:**
>
> This document serves to confirm your need to pay attention to, and comply with, the performance goals reviewed today, November 1, and outlined below. Today's meeting was called because you have not met the goals we mutually agree on in our meeting on March 4. As you know, these goals and the continuing issue were again brought to your attention in the written notification I issued on July 10. Your continuing non-compliance is entirely unacceptable.
>
> Specifically, in our March 4 meeting, we agreed on three goals:
>
> - Call on ten new clients each quarter.
> - Increase your plan achievement by 95 percent.
> - Complete a weekly report detailing your sales calls and interactions with customer service.
>
> To date, you have failed to meet all three. You have called on an average of seven new clients, your plan-achievement percent stands at 91 percent, and you failed to file a weekly report for six weeks total—the weeks of May 1, May 29, June 24, September 4, September 25, and October 16. This level of performance cannot continue.
>
> As of this date, November 1, you are being placed on a final for failure to meet our mutually agree-on goals. In order to continue with your employment, you must:
>
> - Call on ten new clients each quarter.

(Continued)

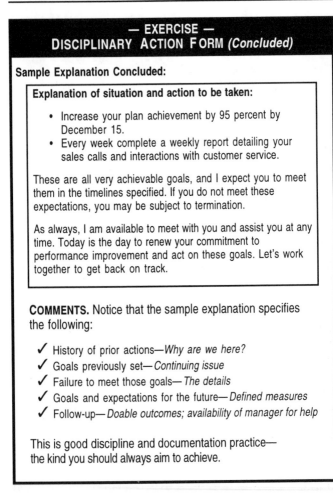

— EXERCISE —
DISCIPLINARY ACTION FORM *(Concluded)*

Sample Explanation Concluded:

> **Explanation of situation and action to be taken:**
>
> - Increase your plan achievement by 95 percent by December 15.
> - Every week complete a weekly report detailing your sales calls and interactions with customer service.
>
> These are all very achievable goals, and I expect you to meet them in the timelines specified. If you do not meet these expectations, you may be subject to termination.
>
> As always, I am available to meet with you and assist you at any time. Today is the day to renew your commitment to performance improvement and act on these goals. Let's work together to get back on track.

COMMENTS. Notice that the sample explanation specifies the following:

✓ History of prior actions—*Why are we here?*
✓ Goals previously set—*Continuing issue*
✓ Failure to meet those goals—*The details*
✓ Goals and expectations for the future—*Defined measures*
✓ Follow-up—*Doable outcomes; availability of manager for help*

This is good discipline and documentation practice—the kind you should always aim to achieve.

Termination:
Procedure and Documentation

TERMINATION REQUIRES the utmost attention to safe procedure and detailed documentation. Wrongful-discharge lawsuits and charges of discrimination are common responses to termination, and they are costly in terms of litigation expense and negative impact on an organization. The ultimate goal of any company is, of course, to avoid termination by effectively facilitating performance improvement. However, it is unrealistic to assume that improvement will always occur—not all employees will be dedicated to excellence. And even the best disciplinary practices cannot prevent offenses that require immediate termination. The most an organization can do is establish a consistent procedure for termination, such as the one in this book, and make sure it is meticulously followed and documented whenever termination is necessary.

In this chapter, we will initially focus on performance-related termination and its procedure and documentation; then we will turn our attention to immediate termination. A list of termination pitfalls and pratfalls is also included.

PERFORMANCE-RELATED TERMINATION: PROCEDURE AND DOCUMENTATION

If you have legitimately reached this drastic step of the disciplinary process, you have exhausted all the possibilities afforded by verbal, written, and final discussions. You have coached the employee, followed up, and found the employee entirely unwilling or unable to modify the problem behavior. You have documented the disciplinary process faithfully, using the proper formats and ensuring your documentation is clear and understandable. You have reached the point where you have no other choice. Anything less than the above means you have *not* reached this step legitimately and should reconsider your decision to terminate.

Preparation

When indeed termination is necessary, be ready to meet with the employee, and to document that meeting. Begin with these steps:

Preparation Steps

1. *Check your state's rules for termination,* and be prepared to follow those rules. For example, California and some other states require that you give the employee his or her final paycheck when you terminate.

2. *Check your organization's guidelines for termination,* and observe them. If your guidelines set forth procedures which have not been followed, it is premature to terminate.

3. *Secure a third party for meeting attendance.* I recommend you never terminate without a third party, preferably another manager, in attendance. This individual helps you maintain control in a potentially volatile situation and serves as a witness to what was said and, just as important, what was not said.

4. *Set a meeting date and time, and notify the employee.* Make sure you set a date and time when the third-party individual is available.

5. *Prepare good, thorough notes.* As for any disciplinary meeting, your notes are valuable memory and documentation aids. Pay especially close attention to the specifics, noting the history of the violation in detail. Again, organize the notes well, so you can actually use them during the meeting.

6. *Rehearse the material several times.* Know the material and what you are going to say.

7. *Develop a plan for the unexpected.* As with any disciplinary meeting, ask yourself

"What if . . ." and come up with a plan for dealing with it.

8. *Document.* Be sure your third party records the employee's comments. Your attention is best focused on the employee.

9. *Prepare meeting room.* Select a quiet, private office. Place chairs in the center of the room, away from the desk. Unplug or unhook the telephone just before the meeting. If any office windows face a work area, close the blinds.

Meeting Procedure

Do not view this meeting as one in which you must tailor your reasoning to the employee. Your reasons should be readily apparent if you and the employee have been working together for some time on changing the behavior. State your case, emphasizing past discussions, and end the session. For example:

> *We are here today because of your failure to meet the objectives we set in our verbal discussion on [date], our written discussion on [date], and our final discussion on [date]. As you know, in our last meeting we agreed that our next course of action would be termination. We have reached that stage.*

This is not the time for education or motivation: that time is now past. The only exception is if the employee presents new information or facts that must be investigated. Due process will not be served until the investigation is completed. The process must be exhausted before termination.

Documentation

Your documentation needs for termination differ from those for earlier disciplinary-process steps, as you are no longer focusing your efforts on problem solving and performance improvement. For this step, you need to prepare a letter of termination in advance of your meeting with the employee. The department head, Human Resources, and your legal department should review the letter *before* you give it to the employee at the meeting. The letter should state the reasons for termination as spelled out in your previous verbal, written, and final discussions. This is not a time to get creative. Use clear, direct language to stress that:

- The employee continued the unwanted behavior

- The company expended considerable time and effort on trying to change the behavior

- The employee chose to ignore the company's efforts and input

Place the emphasis on the employee and his or her non-compliance with the company's effort toward positive change. Some sample statements:

- *Your continued violation of the company's work rules leave the company with no choice except to terminate our employment relationship.*

- *Your continued disregard for the company's input on your continuing performance issue leaves us with no choice except terminating our employment relationship.*

- *Because of your flagrant disregard of our prior discussions, you leave us with no choice except termination, effective immediately.*

- *Because of the extreme and serious nature of your actions, you leave the company with no choice except to terminate the employment relationship.*

- *The company has met with you on several occasions to discuss and assist you in changing your work behavior. You have failed to meet the mutually agreed on goals we set, which leaves the company with no choice but to terminate the employment relationship.*

The sample termination letter on page 120 shows you how it all comes together. Note the continual reference to the employee and his or her refusal to change. This emphasizes the employee has made a conscious decision not to comply. As I mentioned earlier, a manager can only provide the roadmap to change and help the employee reach the destination; the employee must want to change and get to that destination.

Voluntary Termination

On occasion an employee may choose to resign instead of accepting termination. In such a case, ask the person to give the company a letter of resignation stating the reasons for the decision. The employee's letter to you should include a statement acknowledging the employee's desire to leave on his or her own volition. The company can also send to the employee a letter detailing the circumstances surrounding the resignation and confirming the resignation. Both methods help to validate the employee's decision to voluntarily terminate.

A note of caution: Do not be lulled into believing you are "free and clear" of any problems from this point on. There is a doctrine called *constructive discharge* which states, in effect, that the company made the person's environment so intolerable, the person's only alternative was voluntary resignation. However, the company can use the employee's letter to raise reasonable doubt and use it to counter any legal challenge by emphasizing choice on the employee's part and arguing that working conditions were tolerable.

✦ How It All Comes Together ✦

Letter for Performance-Related Termination—Sample

The company has met with you on several occasions to discuss your continuing performance issue.

Specifically, we met on March 3, and I issued a verbal; on May 7, and I issued a written; and again on June 29, at which time you were placed on a final. In each instance, we discussed in detail your failure to improve your overall rate of absenteeism. And in each meeting you gave me your commitment to comply with the goals we mutually established. In total, you have missed over 30 days of work, placing an undue hardship on the department and your coworkers. Since our last meeting, you have once again been absent, displaying a disregard for your stated commitment to change.

This continuing issue can no longer be tolerated. Your continued violation of the company's work rules leave the company with no choice but to terminate our employment relationship.

Obviously, you do not validate the letter of resignation, as it is employee-generated; but you may want to record your acceptance of the resignation, in writing, at the bottom of the letter. Statements you can use include:

- *Per your request, the company accepts your decision to voluntarily terminate your employment.*

120

- *Per your decision, the company will honor your request to voluntarily terminate your employment, effective immediately.*

- *After considerable thought, the company will honor your decision to voluntarily terminate your employment and accepts your letter of resignation.*

- *The company has spent considerable time and effort on working with you on your performance issues. Your decision not to continue working toward positive change is regrettable; however, we will accept your decision to voluntarily resign.*

- *The company will honor your decision to voluntarily leave our employment, effective (date). We wish you the best in your new employment endeavors.*

If you choose this option, give the employee a copy of the letter with your statement on it.

Our final word of caution. If the employee submits a letter of resignation citing uncareful or improper conduct on the part of the company or fellow employees as the reason for his/her resignation, you should conduct a full investigation. It must include making contact with the employee to obtain his/her version of the events. Do not terminate until you are satisfied with your investigation.

Rules of Confidentiality

Follow these rules closely. By ensuring confidentiality of the termination case and documentation, including counseling, you will help protect the company against unfounded claims of retaliation and defamation.

Rules of Confidentiality

- File document where it is completely confidential but easily retrievable.

- Never give the documents to anyone inside the organization unless there is a legitimate reason for the person to see them.

- Never send the documents to anyone outside the organization unless it is subpoenaed. Always consult with your attorney before sending the information. If attorney approves, send only the requested information.

- Never answer queries on the terminated employee over the telephone or in writing. In most instances, provide no more than name, dates of employment, and job title.

- Maintain the documentation for a minimum of five years.

- Never discuss the reasons for termination with anyone who does not have a need to know about them.

Termination Checklist

You should develop a checklist to ensure the company follows a set protocol each and every time an employee leaves the company. It is especially critical that the record is properly stored and that all inquiries about the person's departure are referred to the human resources department.

✓ TERMINATION CHECKLIST

❏ Present final paycheck.

❏ Ask for identification cards, office keys.

❏ Explain COBRA entitlements.*

❏ Notify state employment compensation department.

❏ Refer to Human Resources any external inquiries about the employee's departure.

❏ Notify insurance carrier.

❏ Place documented reason for termination in employee's file, along with all other documented issues.

❏ Place complete employee file in record retention for storage.

❏ Notify security checkpoint(s).

*COBRA (Consolidated Omnibus Budget Reconciliation Act) protects insurance coverage for a specified length of time.

IMMEDIATE TERMINATION: PROCEDURE AND DOCUMENTATION

In the case of a serious, non-performance-related offense, you may choose to immediately terminate the employee, that is, terminate without going through the disciplinary process. Actions that merit such severe consideration, even on a first-time basis, include the following:

- Fighting/Violence
- Theft
- Deliberate destruction of company property
- Sexual harassment
- Use or sale of drugs on company property
- Falsification of company documents
- Bringing weapons on company property

It is a good idea to have a policy in place that details the consequences of such actions. Include the policy in the employee handbook, where all employees can review it. You might even post it on all the company bulletin boards. The policy should state that your list is illustrative only, and is not a complete nor comprehensive list of offenses meriting termination, and that there may be other bases or situations in which the company reserves the right to terminate immediately.

The Need for Proof: Investigation

Never base your decision to terminate on rumor or unsubstantiated claims. Your best defense is to prove the violation was committed—and usually, to substantiate that proof, you must conduct a formal investigation.

You should have a standard investigation method in place in your organization, to ensure consistency of action across cases; and those likely to investigate such violations should be trained in that process. You can use the information in this section either to reinforce the credibility of that process, or as a basis for establishing a standard method.

The Special Case of Firsthand Observation

If your position is one based on firsthand observation—that is, if you caught the person in the act of commiting the violation (e.g., selling drugs)—you have an immediate legal advantage. This is the most defensible position because you have *seen* the violation. There is no hearsay or subjectivity to cloud the issue.

In such a situation, take this course of action:

- Bring the employee into your office or other suitable area.

- Get a witness to stand in, as described earlier in this chapter.

- Terminate the employee; then, for security reasons, have the employee quietly escorted to the exit.

- Document.

- Send the termination letter to the employee via registered mail.

As in the case of performance-related termination, make sure your documentation (termination letter) is reviewed by the department head, Human Resources, and your legal department.

Preliminary Concerns and Investigation Guidelines

Before proceeding with an investigation, make sure an investigation is necessary. To determine its need, ask yourself: *Can I immediately resolve this issue?* Sometimes employees admit they are guilty as accused; at other times, the offense becomes self-evident. For instance, Mary accuses John of sexual harassment, and John admits his actions when you meet with him; or someone reports John has brought a gun on to the premises, and you confirm it when you meet with him. Most of the time, though, you will find that you need to investigate.

Before you begin the investigation, you should suspend the employee. Call the employee into a quiet office, and be forthright in your comments. Use this sample as a guide:

Jim, you were fighting, and we do not tolerate such activity at this company. After I take a statement from you to get your side of the story, you must leave the building. I will call you in three days to let you know our decision on whether to terminate you or reinstate you. I also want you to know I will be interviewing all witnesses to get at the facts of this unfortunate situation.

After you have suspended the employee, follow the guidelines below.

When an Investigation Is Necessary . . .
Who-What-When-Where-Witnesses

- Identify potential witnesses. Who has knowledge of the alleged event?

- Determine who will conduct the investigation. Assign two investigators. Both will record comments to ensure accuracy.

- Formulate your questions. Make sure they are open-ended, that is, designed to elicit responses. For example, "What can you tell me about Mary's sexual harassment claim?"

- Document conversations with interviewees, and take action if warranted (do so in a timely manner).

Once you have gathered this information, it must be reviewed by those who approve terminations (e.g., Human Resources, legal department). If your process calls for more people, get them involved.

Termination Procedure: Notifying and Meeting With the Employee

If your investigation confirms the accusations or events, let the employee know by telephone when to return to work; provide a specific date and time. You may be pressured to give your answer over the phone. I suggest you do not do so. A face-to-face termination meeting is always preferable, as the employee's comments can be documented. You can also hand the employee the letter of termination, an example of which is on page 129.

As for the termination meeting, take the following action:

- Get a witness to attend. This person will document the employee's comments.

- Inform the employee that the investigation has upheld the accusations or events.

- Give the employee the letter of termination.

- For security reasons, escort the employee to the door in an unobstrusive manner. Employees who are escorted by security or in a manner that implies wrongdoing may sue for defamation.

✦ How It All Comes Together ✦

Letter for Immediate Termination—Sample

On Tuesday, June 6, we met with you to suspend your employment pending investigation of the issues concerning an alleged charge of sexual harassment. At that meeting we gave you ample time to explain your actions. Since Tuesday, we have interviewed a number of witnesses, provided by you and the charging party, to sort out the facts of the charge. Our findings confirm the allegation made against you. As a result, and per our sexual-harassment prevention policy, we find it necessary to terminate your employment, effective immediately.

Documentation

The termination letter should be clear and to the point. You need to detail the offense, mention the meeting subsequent to that offense, and stress that an investigation was conducted. For a model, see the sample termination letter I have provided.

PITFALLS AND PRATFALLS OF TERMINATION

As you now know, the decision to terminate is a major undertaking. In order to prevent a mistake, always ask yourself, "Have I forgotten anything that weakens this decision?"

For example, let's say you terminate a female employee for poor job performance and she files a charge of discrimination, stating she was fired only because she is a woman. You check out the employee's records and find her last two performance reviews were not bad. She was rated 3 on a scale of 1 to 5. You further discover she was just given a merit increase only three months ago. How did this happen?

Frankly, it should not have happened. The following list will help you avoid such oversights. Always audit yourself using this list whenever you are thinking of terminating someone.

Also, I recommend you develop a policy that limits raises, transfers, and promotions, and include it in your employee handbook and company policy and procedures manual. When an employee's performance has improved, as defined by the rule of deactivation, you can reinstate the privilege. Generally speaking, a process to "limit" begins at the written notification level.

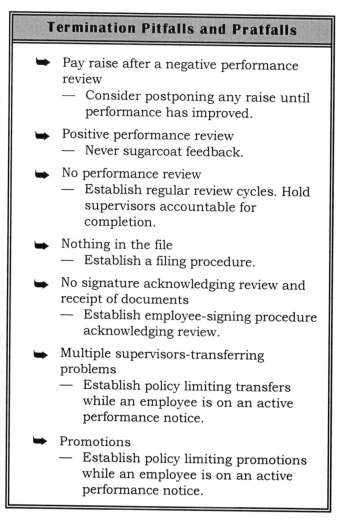

Termination Pitfalls and Pratfalls

➡ Pay raise after a negative performance review
  — Consider postponing any raise until performance has improved.

➡ Positive performance review
  — Never sugarcoat feedback.

➡ No performance review
  — Establish regular review cycles. Hold supervisors accountable for completion.

➡ Nothing in the file
  — Establish a filing procedure.

➡ No signature acknowledging review and receipt of documents
  — Establish employee-signing procedure acknowledging review.

➡ Multiple supervisors-transferring problems
  — Establish policy limiting transfers while an employee is on an active performance notice.

➡ Promotions
  — Establish policy limiting promotions while an employee is on an active performance notice.

Specific Problems and Solutions

AS WE HAVE SEEN, employee behavioral issues tend to fall into either of two categories: the process-amenable problem and the serious offense. The four-step disciplinary process is the best method for problems traced to a gap in execution; the training process is the best for problems caused by a gap in comprehension. The former (which have been our main focus in this book) include absenteeism, tardiness, poor performance, and minor work-rule violations. Suspension, formal investigation and, possibly, immediate termination form the course of action for serious offenses. They include fighting, theft, drug use, and forms of harassment.

In this chapter, we will focus on guidelines for managing two process-amenable problems, absenteeism and tardiness, and two serious offenses, fighting and harassment. We will also take a look at preventing problems by putting people first.

Remember: use the following guidelines, and any others in this guidebook, in conjunction with your company's policy and procedure for such issues.

ABSENTEEISM AND TARDINESS

These two problems are common headaches for managers. There are two keys to resolving them:

1. Address the problem early on, when you first notice it. The average employee misses around five days of work a year; any more than that is an issue worth discussing.

2. Look for patterns in the problem behavior. Monday and Friday absences, which create a three-day weekend, are common.

The guidelines below are applicable to both problems. "Cures" specific to each problem will follow.

General Guidelines: Absenteeism and Tardiness

Maintain records.

- Keep accurate attendance records. Look for patterns; Mondays and Fridays, special events or holidays, repetitive reasons for absence.
- Keep records of instances of tardiness.

Notify problem employee in a timely fashion.

- Make the employee aware that excessive absenteeism or tardiness is unacceptable. Define excessive. Follow precedent.
- Solve small problems before they become big ones.

Use disciplinary process for violations.

- Follow disciplinary process—verbal, written, and final discussions—when problems arise.

Practice preventive methods.

- Establish expectations at hiring date.
- Demonstrate appreciation for good attendance and punctuality. Publicize the excellence of those who keep to the rules.

The Unexcused Absence

To help "cure" the unexcused absence, establish a clearly stated call-in policy. An effective policy will state the employee must notify the company, by phone, in the half-hour period before the shift's start. The call must be received by the employee's supervisor or someone serving in a management capacity; calls to coworkers, or notification via coworkers, do not meet the policy requirements.

Remedy: The Unexcused Absence

- Establish a clear policy for absenteeism.

  - All absences must be reported within a half hour before start of workshift.
  - Three consecutive days of "no call, no show" result in termination documented as job abandonment.

— Isolated instances of unexcused absenteeism merit disciplinary action.

- Enforce the policy.
  — Again, timely action for violations is crucial.
  — Be consistent across employees when enforcing policy. Avoid exceptions to policy.

Tardiness

Always use a step process for tardiness to give the employee ample time to correct the problem. It is generally useful to spell out your expectations in the verbal discussion. For example, "The next instance may result in a written discussion."

Remedy: Tardiness

- Determine acceptable and unacceptable rates of tardiness. Ensure employees know what they are.
- Always use the disciplinary process for tardiness.
- Note patterns of tardiness and take immediate action.
- Discuss with the employee . . .
  — your course of action
  — the reasons for the tardy behavior
  — how to resolve the problem

- Ensure consistency from one employee to another.
- Value punctuality in employees.

Limitation

When reviewing the possibility of discipline for absenteeism and tardiness always consider whether the employee's absences are protected by law. The Family Medical Leave Act and the Americans with Disabilities Act, along with Workers Compensation Statutes and Pregnancy Leave Statutes may limit your ability to discipline. Know the reasons behind the absences before you take disciplinary action.

PHYSICAL ACTS OF VIOLENCE: FIGHTING

There are four keys to dealing with this type of serious offense:

1. Interview all witnesses to the incident. Who started what is important, especially if penalties are set at different levels.

2. Suspend both parties while you investigate the situation, with reinstatement pending the investigation results.

3. Do not telephone either employee with the results of your investigation. Bring them back to the work site for confidential discussion and action.

4. If different penalties are handed out, be sure you have solid reasons for them and cannot be accused of inconsistency of application.

Normally, discharge is upheld on a first-time basis in cases of fighting and other violent acts. Be sure you have all the facts before taking such extreme action.

In investigating the situation, be sure to find answers to these questions:

- What specifically caused the action?
- Was either party acting solely in self-defense?
- Were there witnesses to the actions? If so, what did they see?
- Is this repetitive behavior?

In general, if your investigation finds that both parties are guilty, termination is the likely response. Should your investigation reveal that one party tried to avoid the confrontation and acted in self-defense, then your likely response is to terminate only the aggressor. The bottom line is, the facts and your own good judgment will dictate your response. If you have any doubts whatsoever about the appropriateness of your response, seek the counsel of your supervisor, Human Resources, and your legal department. As detailed earlier, never make a decision to terminate on your own.

Document and follow procedures as you have studied in this guidebook.

HARASSMENT

This is a particularly difficult charge to deal with—and one that is a big issue in today's workplace. I recommend that you investigate all claims of harassment, and that you do so in detail, following a standard procedure for investigation.

Types of Harassment

Generally, there are two types: *quid pro quo* and *hostile environment.* The first is translatable as "this for that" or "something for something," and usually, in its most negative context, it has a sexual connotation. Examples: "Go out on a date with me, and I'll see to it you get a raise," and "Sleep with me, and I'll see to it you're promoted." Comments such as this are extremely serious and must not be taken lightly.

The second type, hostile environment, is not as cut-and-dried. Here a supervisor (or an employee) is charged by an employee with having created an environment that is so intolerable the employee cannot work. Both this and quid pro quo normally require some investigative work.

Suggested Investigative Procedure

The following is a sound approach to the investigation of this offense. It is key to interview anyone identified as the harasser or as a witness to the incident. It is also important to interview any employee identified as a victim of the same conduct.

Investigative Procedure

- Assign investigative team.
- Separately interview the charging employee, the alleged harasser, and all witnesses.
- Examine all data.
- Determine whether company policy has been violated.
- Decide on corrective action.
- Communicate the decision to the parties involved, that is, the charging party and the alleged harasser.
- Follow up to ensure the harassment is stopped, or discharge the harasser.

Note that harassment, like fighting, is an offense where termination can be upheld on a first-time basis. It depends on the extent, frequency, and nature of the harassment.

The flow chart on page 142 highlights the three questions of prime importance: Is the issue harassment? Does it require further investigation? Is the claim substantiated?

When interviewing the charging party, always offer the use of an employee assistance program (EAP). Also, provide a copy of the company's harassment prevention policy. This helps to establish a "good faith" effort on the part of the company. Questions to ask the employee during your interview include:

- Who harassed you?
- Were there any witnesses?
- Why do you feel you were harassed? Please provide specifics.
- Has it happened before? When?
- Where did it take place?
- What was your reaction to the harassment?

Be sure to note the answers to these questions, and, of couse, always follow them up with appropriate action.

FIGURE 5. Harassment Investigation Procedure

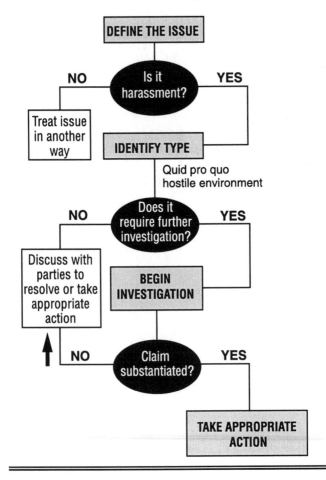

THE BEST SOLUTION: PEOPLE FIRST

This book is about change, and change is not an easy task. It is built on a foundation of trust, and must be part of the organizational culture and openly embraced by everyone. You can help to establish such a culture by monitoring your actions and keeping to the simple rule of "practice what you preach."

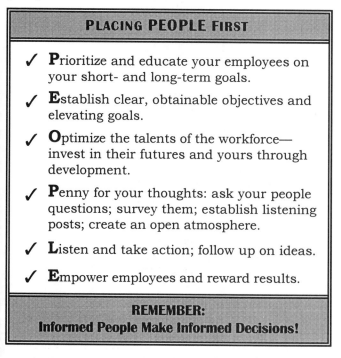

PLACING PEOPLE FIRST

✓ **P**rioritize and educate your employees on your short- and long-term goals.

✓ **E**stablish clear, obtainable objectives and elevating goals.

✓ **O**ptimize the talents of the workforce—invest in their futures and yours through development.

✓ **P**enny for your thoughts: ask your people questions; survey them; establish listening posts; create an open atmosphere.

✓ **L**isten and take action; follow up on ideas.

✓ **E**mpower employees and reward results.

REMEMBER:
Informed People Make Informed Decisions!

I have found that if you place people first, they will place you first as well—and you can prevent most problems from developing. How do you make it happen? By remembering the PEOPLE anagram and *putting it into practice.* You may find that you seldom need to worry about taking disciplinary action at all.

Appendices

APPENDIX A

A Ready Reference to the Guidebook	
➥ *If you want to . . .*	➥ *then see . . .*
• Treat discipline as a method to effect positive change	Introduction
• Establish a four-step process —Verbal, written, final	Chapter 2
• Distinguish between comprehension and execution	Chapter 2
• Use phases to ensure consistency — Investigate, Deliberate, Adjudicate, Administrate, Evaluate	Chapter 2
• Establish ground rules — Process, ACT, Equal Treatment, Communication, Open-Flame Analogy, Rule of Relevance, Right of Appeal	Chapter 3
• Use PEP and TALKTALK	Chapter 4
• Use language effectively	Chapter 5
• Use termination procedures	Chapter 6
• Look into problems and solutions	Chapter 7
Document! Document! Document!	

APPENDIX B

Optional Exercises

These exercises will promote team building, idea sharing, and open communication among the members of your organization or smaller work groups. They will also reinforce, through repeated use, some of the tenets in this guidebook while also generating a sense of understanding about the disciplinary process.

1. 360-Degree Feedback

Develop a form you can use to ask your employees their opinions about your ability to communicate.

- Are you effective?
- Are you informative?
- Do you actively and regularly coach?

Have the employees respond anonymously. Consider using checklists or similar formats that do not require handwriting (thus better ensuring anonymity). Take the input and problem-solve any communication issues with employees.

2. Manager's Coaching Profile

Use "The Manager's Coaching Self-Profile" in Chapter 1 as an assessment tool that employees can use to give you feedback on your coaching. Their insights might point you in the direction of self-improvement.

3. Disciplinary Action Form

Let your employees critique the disciplinary action form. It will instill ownership and create awareness of it and its intent. Your employees may provide additional items of perceived importance.

4. Case Participation

Let your employees work on the exercise "The Case of John Wasastar" in Chapter 2. It reinforces the belief that discipline is necessary in some instances.

5. Audit

Let your employees audit your current discipline program against this book. For example, do you have anything similar to a progressive step process, the five *R*'s of change, an employment-at-will statement, or a methodology to distinguish execution from comprehension? Let the employees define the gaps in the program and develop an action plan on what the organization can do to bridge those gaps.

Index

About the Author

TERRY L. FITZWATER is managing partner of FLC Leadership Consulting. His firm specializes in employee relations and organization development. Prior to consulting he spent over 17 years as a human resource executive with a Fortune 100 company. He is a frequent speaker on various employee relations topics and an adjunct faculty member for a local university instructing management classes. For further information on discipline and documentation, as well as other topics, you can contact Mr. Fitzwater at (916) 791-7938 or (916) 791-0692; E-mail, www.tfitzh2o@quiknet.com.